first time
GARMENT FITTING

THE ABSOLUTE BEGINNER'S GUIDE

LEARN BY DOING ✳ STEP-BY-STEP BASICS + PROJECTS

by Sarah Veblen

Creative Publishing
international

To Charles Kleibacker, for his life's work of keeping the craft alive.
And to Bonnie, who was there for me every step of the way.

Brimming with creative inspiration, how-to projects, and useful information to enrich your everyday life, Quarto Knows is a favorite destination for those pursuing their interests and passions. Visit our site and dig deeper with our books into your area of interest: Quarto Creates, Quarto Cooks, Quarto Homes, Quarto Lives, Quarto Drives, Quarto Explores, Quarto Gifts, or Quarto Kids.

© 2018 Quarto Publishing Group USA Inc.
Text and projects/patterns © 2012 Sarah Veblen
Photography © 2012 Quarto Publishing Group USA Inc.

First published in 2018 by Creative Publishing international, an imprint of The Quarto Group, 100 Cummings Center, Suite 265-D, Beverly, MA 01915, USA.
T (978) 282-9590 F (978) 283-2742 QuartoKnows.com

Creative Publishing international titles are also available at discount for retail, wholesale, promotional, and bulk purchase. For details, contact the Special Sales Manager by email at specialsales@quarto.com or by mail at The Quarto Group, Attn: Special Sales Manager, 100 Cummings Center, Suite 265-D, Beverly, MA 01915, USA.

ISBN: 978-1-58923-962-3

Digital edition published in 2018

The content for this book was originally published in *The Complete Photo Guide to Perfect Fitting* (CPi, 2012) by Sarah Veblen.

Library of Congress Cataloging-in-Publication Data available

Design and Page Layout: Megan Jones Design
Photography: Michael DeFilippi
Illustration: Bonnie Veblen

Printed in USA

contents

preface

There's an aura of beauty about a woman wearing clothes that fit her well, regardless of her figure and facial features. Her clothes create a sense of balance and proportion for her body, which is flattering to her and visually pleasing to others. She's definitely wearing her clothes, rather than her clothes wearing her.

Although styles change and clothing fads come and go, the hallmarks of well-fitting clothes remain the same:

* There are no unintended pulls or folds in the fabric.

* The fabric falls smoothly over the body.

* The garment is proportionate to the wearer's body.

* The cut of the garment is flattering.

When wearing clothes that fit, we not only present ourselves better, but we feel more comfortable. And when we feel at ease in our clothes, we think more clearly, interact with other people better, and approach the day's challenges and pleasures with a healthier attitude. There is no need to feel squirmy in your clothes, counting the minutes until you can get home and change into your comfy sweats. It all starts with getting a good fit.

Fitting is complicated, in part because it doesn't stand alone. Rather, it must be tackled within the larger framework of all that is required to make a garment, from design to pattern development. To achieve success, you must have the following:

1 A fitting method to follow

2 An understanding of good fitting practices

3 An understanding of good patternmaking practices

4 The ability to recognize specific fitting issues

5 The ability to put these specific issues within the context of the garment as a whole

This book is organized so that the information builds from one section to the next. In the first and second sections, I describe the conceptual foundation. In the third section, I provide detailed information for making fitting changes to your pattern. And in the final section, I show how to fit a skirt, a bodice with darts, and a bodice with shoulder princess seams.

Even though fitting is complicated, with patience and guidance, everyone can learn to fit.

FITTING FUNDAMENTALS

Being a competent fitter requires both a conceptual and a practical understanding of the fitting process. Skipping the concepts and going straight to the fitting examples is like trying to build a house without first laying its foundation. Just as the house will develop cracks, your fitting will have weaknesses, which will cause confusion and less-than-perfect results.

understanding fit

Any skill requires training. Fitting requires training the eye to recognize what good fit is and what indicates a poor fit. For example, a novice often doesn't notice drag lines until they are pointed out. With practice, the eye becomes trained first to see the obvious fitting problems and eventually then to discern nuances. A good way to train your eye is to observe people's clothes wherever you go, from your work environment to stops at the grocery store.

WHY FITTING IS COMPLICATED

Once the fitting problem is identified, it must be corrected. This requires knowing how to manipulate the cloth. However, the fitting problem cannot be dealt with out of context; it must be solved within the framework of the garment as a whole. In addition, the cloth must be manipulated in a manner that allows the change to be made in the pattern. As your fitting skills improve, your knowledge of pattern work will improve as well due to the interrelationship between fitting and pattern manipulation.

Obtaining a good fit is a process, rarely a one-shot experience. It takes time, patience, and usually multiple muslins to develop a perfect fit. Most sewers think the process is worthwhile, since the end result is that perfectly fitting pattern you've dreamed of.

Fitting yourself is possible but often time consuming. Accurately assessing a muslin on your own body is more difficult than making good observations on someone else. It's helpful to have a dress form that reflects your body; working with a fitting buddy can help even more. Two sets of eyes are useful when learning to identify fitting problems, and you can collaborate on figuring out the best solution. Plus, you can fit each other.

EACH INDIVIDUAL IS UNIQUE

Since no two bodies are exactly the same, fitting requires individualized problem solving. Fitting instructions will get you started, but they are generalized descriptions of a situation and a typical solution. You must then apply this information to the person being fitted. This requires experimenting with and interpreting the fitting instructions. Fitting is easier and more successful when you work with the cloth on the individual's body rather than insisting that a fitting "rule" be applied in a preordained manner.

Although picture-perfect bodies can depict standardized fitting solutions, very few of us have such bodies. This book is comprised of real fitting situations that are characteristic of typical fitting issues. The models are ordinary people with everyday lumps and bumps. Your own body might not be represented by these particular models, but you will find fitting examples throughout the book that are similar to your fitting problems.

In addition to finding solutions to fitting issues, a good fitter also needs a way to reflect on and approach the problems. This book provides a methodology that will help you interpret specific fitting examples and then apply the information to your own fitting issues, leading you to the best solution for your situation. The end result is beautifully fitting clothes.

pattern and fitting basics

Commercial patterns provide a lot of information to help the sewer make an educated selection when choosing a pattern and to assist the sewer when making the garment. Understanding the pattern envelope and its contents is the first step toward using patterns successfully.

FINDING YOUR WAY AROUND A PATTERN

Almost all commercial patterns include a guide sheet that includes a list of pattern pieces, a description of pieces to use for specific views, fabric cutting layouts, seam allowance information, a key to reading the illustrations (how elements such as the right side and wrong side of the fabric are depicted), and step-by-step directions. Some patterns provide a short glossary of sewing terms, and some have helpful design tips.

In addition to these elements, some pattern envelopes also provide information such as a difficulty rating based on the sewing techniques required to make the garment, recommendations of figure types for the garment style, and stretch guides for knits-only patterns.

Remember, a pattern is a tool for you to use, not a dictum that you must follow precisely. It's important to view the information that the pattern supplies within the context of your knowledge about sewing, fabric, and pattern work.

The Pattern Envelope Front

Garment depiction is a fashion illustration or a photograph of the garment. Some patterns provide both.

Views show garment variations and options.

Size indicates size or sizes included. Multi-sized patterns usually print all cutting lines on the same tissue.

The Pattern Envelope Back

Line drawings often convey more information than the illustration or photo on the front of the pattern, because they provide style lines (seam placement) and fitting elements such as darts.

Descriptive caption describes how the garment is cut (loose or close to the body) and general stylistic elements of the garment.

Finished garment measurements also indicate how the garment is cut. For example, hemline circumferences are usually given. Some pattern companies provide more information than others.

Size chart lists standardized measurements and correlating pattern sizes.

Notions list indicates items such as shoulder pads and buttons required for the pattern, including size specifications.

Fabric recommendations are suggested fabrics for the pattern's garment(s); use this information as a guide in conjunction with your own knowledge of fabrics.

Yardage chart indicates how much fabric to buy, usually with two different pattern layouts: with nap (all pattern pieces are oriented in the same direction) and without nap (the pattern pieces are oriented to use the least amount of fabric).

The Pattern Pieces

Dot, **triangle**, or **square symbols** are match points for adjoining pattern pieces. If you think of the pattern as a puzzle, these symbols help you put the puzzle together correctly.

Grainline arrow specifies the orientation of the pattern piece on the fabric. Grainline arrows usually indicate the length-of-grain and therefore should be placed parallel to the selvage of the fabric. Grainline is extremely important because it is what makes your garments hang correctly.

Placement lines indicate the position for elements such pockets, buttonholes, and trims.

Double line provides an appropriate place to lengthen or shorten the pattern with minimal disruption of the pattern's style lines.

Finished garment measurements are sometimes provided for the bust, waist, and hip. This is useful information in determining how much ease is included in the pattern.

GARMENT SILHOUETTES AND EASE

Clothes create a silhouette on the body, falling into one of three general categories:

1 Clothes cut close or fairly close to the body create a fitted silhouette. Stylistically, tailored garments that have enough ease to move comfortably but without excess fabric fall into this category. Eveningwear and formal clothes can also be in this category. And depending on what is currently popular, trendy clothes might be cut quite close to the body.

2 Clothes cut with more ease but without being loose and baggy create a relaxed silhouette. Stylistically, these clothes often look more casual than tailored garments. They run the gamut, including office wear, everyday clothes, and weekend favorites.

3 Clothes that incorporate even more ease create a loose silhouette. Stylistically, the fullness can look proportionate on the body if the volume of fabric is well controlled. It can also look baggy and oversized, which periodically is popular.

It's important to be comfortable in your clothes, but comfort is not solely dependent on how much ease is in your garment. A very large garment can be uncomfortable and restrictive just as easily as a garment that's too small. Fabric selection impacts the way a garment feels on the body. But the biggest key to comfort is good fit.

| 1 | 2 | 3A | 3B |

Fitted silhouette   Relaxed silhouette   Controlled fullness silhouette   Loose silhouette

Two Kinds of Garment Ease

Garment ease refers to the difference between the finished measurements of the garment and the measurements of the wearer's body. With woven fabrics, the garment needs to be at least somewhat larger than the body; otherwise we cannot move in our clothes. This difference is referred to as wearing ease.

Some garments are intentionally bigger than the wearer's body in order to create a specific look. When a garment is purposely styled to be noticeably larger than the body, this is referred to as design ease.

A 1960s tent dress is a perfect example of design ease. There is a great deal more ease in the hip area than is needed to move comfortably in the garment. It is precisely this design ease that creates the style of the dress.

With knit fabrics, the garment's finished measurements often equal the wearer's body measurements, because the knit structure and its ability to give provide the wearing ease. Garments such as activewear and bathing suits that are made of stretch knits (knits with spandex) have negative ease. In this case, the garment's finished measurements are smaller than the wearer's body measurements, because the fit is partially obtained as the fabric stretches around the body.

1960s tent dress

CHOOSING A PATTERN SIZE

It's rare that a commercial pattern is ideal for your figure, because these patterns are developed for a standardized body. Some pattern companies base their patterns on a specific figure type; this is convenient if you find a pattern company that uses a figure similar to yours. For most women, however, commercial patterns are simply a tool—a good starting place for developing a pattern that fits.

Pattern envelopes provide a measurement/size chart to help you choose a pattern size. While using this chart is simple, there are a number of variables to consider in addition to your body measurements when selecting a pattern size.

Taking Your Measurements

Accurate body measurements are an essential starting point. Wear the undergarments that you normally would with the garment you intend to sew. Undergarments that fit well make the fitting process easier and the final garment more attractive. When taking measurements, assume a normal stance; do not pull the tape tight, but have it rest lightly on the body.

* **High bust/chest.** Measure directly under the arms, across the chest (above the full bust), and across the back, keeping the tape straight across the back.

* **Bust/full bust.** Measure over the fullest part of the bust and across the back, keeping the tape straight and parallel to the floor.

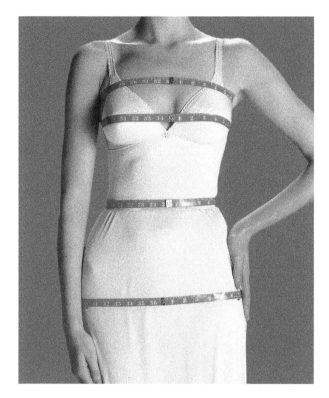

* **Waist.** Measure the natural waist, which is the smallest part of the torso, even if you usually wear your garments lower. A narrow elastic tied around the waist will seek the smallest part of the torso.

* **Hip.** Measure the fullest part of the hip/buttock, keeping the tape parallel to the floor. Use the abdominal measurement or a high, full thigh measurement if it is greater than the hip/buttock measurement.

WHERE'S MY WAIST?

Although most people think of their waist as where they prefer the top of their skirts and pants to rest, the waist by definition is the smallest part of the torso. Many women wear skirts and pants not at the natural waist but sitting lower on the torso, often just resting on the top of the hip bone or at the navel. Style trends often have the "waist" even lower on the pelvis. Commercial patterns are developed with the waist at the smallest part of the torso, unless the pattern specifies otherwise (for instance, "1½" [3.8 cm] below waist" might be printed near the top of a skirt pattern). For fitting and pattern development purposes, think of a lowered waistline as a stylistic element.

Which Measurements to Use?

Having an accurate set of measurements allows you to go to the next step: deciding what size pattern to buy. Start with the size chart on the pattern envelope to determine which size the pattern company recommends.

For skirts and pants (bottoms), use your full hip measurement, or the abdomen or high thigh measurement if it is larger than the hip/buttock measurement.

For blouses and jackets (tops), choosing a pattern size is more complicated, because most commercial pattern companies develop their patterns for a B-cup size. Some specially marked patterns provide multiple cup sizes, and others are sized for a full figure.

Many women whose bust is larger than a B cup prefer to use the high bust/chest measurement to select the pattern size, because the full bust measurement puts them into a pattern size that is disproportionate to their frame. The smaller size pattern better fits their frame, and a full bust adjustment is made to the pattern to accommodate the larger cup size. If the full bust measurement is used to select the pattern size, then the shoulder width and armhole will likely need to be adjusted and made smaller. Both approaches are valid; use the one that makes the most sense to you.

For women with an A-cup size, the same situation exists but in reverse. If the full bust measurement is used to select the pattern size, the shoulder width and upper torso length will likely need to be adjusted and made larger. Alternatively, if the high bust/chest measurement is used, a small bust adjustment will need to be made.

Determining Your Cup Size

Subtract the chest measurement from the full bust measurement.

A cup = 1" (2.5 cm) or less
B cup = 1¼" to 2" (3.2 to 5.1 cm)
C cup = 2¼" to 3" (5.7 to 7.6 cm)
D cup = 3¼" to 4" (8.3 to 10.2 cm)
DD cup = 4¼" to 5" (10.8 to 12.7 cm)

Using a Standard Measurement/Size Chart

Pattern sizes are standardized among the major pattern companies, but these sizes bear no relation to ready-to-wear sizes. To select a pattern size based on your bust measurement, read across the "bust" line until you come to your measurement; then read up to find the pattern size.

Use the same method if using a hip measurement. If your body measurement is between two sizes, considering the variables described in this chapter will help you make a logical pattern size selection. Remember, the pattern is just a tool to help you get started.

FIGURE SIZE CHART

MISSES'/MISS PETITE

Sizes	4	6	8	10	12	14	16	18	20	22	24	26
Sizes-European	30	32	34	36	38	40	42	44	46	48	50	52
Bust	29½"	30½"	31½"	32½"	34"	36"	38"	40"	42"	44"	46"	48"
Centimeters	75	78	80	83	87	92	97	102	107	112	117	122
Waist	22"	23"	24"	25"	26½"	28"	30"	32"	34"	37"	39"	41½"
Centimeters	56	58	61	64	67	71	76	81	87	94	99	105.5
Hip – 9" (23 cm) below waist	31½"	32½"	33½"	34½"	36"	38"	40"	42"	44"	46"	48"	50"
Centimeters	80	83	85	88	92	97	102	107	112	117	122	127
Back Waist Length	15¼"	15½"	15¾"	16"	16¼"	16½"	16¾"	17"	17¼"	17⅜"	17½"	17¾"
Centimeters	38.5	39.5	40	40.5	41.5	42	42.5	43	44	44	44.5	45
Petite-Back Waist Length	14¼"	14½"	14¾"	15"	15¼"	15½"	15¾"	16"	16¼"	16⅜"	16½"	16⅝"
Centimeters	36	37	37.5	38	39	39.5	40	40.5	41	41.5	42	42

FIGURE SIZE CHART

WOMEN'S/WOMEN'S PETITE

Sizes	18W	20W	22W	24W	26W	28W	30W	32W
Sizes-European	44	46	48	50	52	54	56	58
Bust	40"	42"	44"	46"	48"	50"	52"	54"
Centimeters	101.5	106.5	112	117	122	127	132	137
Waist	33"	35"	37"	39"	41½"	44"	46½"	49"
Centimeters	84	89	94	99	105.5	112	118	124
Hip – 9" (23 cm) below waist	42"	44"	46"	48"	50"	52"	54"	56"
Centimeters	106.5	112	117	122	127	132	137	142
Back Waist Length	17⅛"	17¼"	17⅜"	17½"	17⅝"	17¾"	17⅞"	18"
Centimeters	43.5	44	44	44.5	45	45	45.5	46
Petite-Back Waist Length	16⅛"	16¼"	16⅜"	16½"	16⅝"	16¾"	16⅞"	17"
Centimeters	41	41.5	41.5	42	42	42.5	43	43

EASE CHART

		Close Fitting	Fitted	Semi Fitted	Loose Fitting	Very Loose Fitting
Bust Area	**Dresses**	0 to 2⅞" (0 to 7.3 cm)	3" to 4" (7.6.2 to 10 cm)	4⅛" to 5" (10.5 to 12.7 cm)	5⅛" to 8" (13 to 20.3 cm)	Over 8" (20.3 cm)
	Jackets		3¾" to 4¼" (9.5 to 10.8 cm)	4⅜" to 5¾" (11.1 to 14.6 cm)	5⅞" to 10" (14.9 to 25.4 cm)	Over 10" (25.4 cm)
	Coats		5¼" to 6¾" (13.3 to 17.2 cm)	6⅞" to 8" (17.5 to 20.3 cm)	8⅛" to 12" (20.7 to 30.5 cm)	Over 12" (30.5 cm)
Hips	**Pants/Skirts**	0 to 1⅞" (0 to 4.8 cm)	2 to 3" (5.1 to 7.6 cm)	3⅛" to 4" (7.9 to 10.2 cm)	4⅛" to 6" (10.5 to 15.2 cm)	Over 6" (15.2 cm)

Other Variables in Selecting a Pattern Size

The amount of ease built in to a pattern affects the way the garment fits. Some patterns include a garment description, which indicates how much ease there is. For instance, a garment might be described as semifitted or loose fitting. However, these terms are imprecise—they describe a range of ease, as seen from the ease chart on the previous page.

The garment rendering or photograph on the pattern envelope also depicts how fitted or loose the garment is intended to be. Unfortunately, these illustrations and photographs do not always accurately reflect the amount of ease in the garment.

Finished garment measurements on either the pattern envelope or the pattern tissue are the most helpful, because they tell you precisely how much ease has been incorporated into the pattern. Simply subtract your body measurement from the finished garment measurement, and the result is how much ease the garment will have on your body. Deciding how much wearing ease and design ease you would like in your garment will guide you in choosing a pattern size.

PATTERN SELECTION

Altering the length of many patterns is very simple, and most patterns provide lengthen/shorten lines for your convenience. Adjusting a pattern's circumference is more difficult. Therefore, select a pattern size that will be close to your desired circumference (wearing ease + design ease), even if you know you will need to alter the length.

Wearing Ease Recommendations

Wearing ease recommendations also vary. For instance, the Butterick chart lists 3" to 4" (7.6 to 10. 2 cm) of ease in the bust for garments in the fitted silhouette category, whereas I find less is necessary. How much wearing ease to include is a matter of personal preference. However, many women find that they need less wearing ease in a garment that fits well compared to a garment that does not fit well.

I recommend the following ease amounts for garments in the fitted silhouette category when the garment fits well. For the hip and the full bust, 1½" to 2" (3.8 to 5.1 cm) for a slender figure, and 2" to 3" (5.1 to 7.6 cm) for a full figure is adequate and comfortable. The waist depends on personal preference; some women like a bit of ease (perhaps ½" to 1" [1.3 to 2.5 cm]), while others actually like negative ease.

tools for pattern work and fitting

A few specialized tools are handy when fitting muslins and adjusting patterns. Since people work more efficiently when tools are comfortable in their hands, try different pencils and paper scissors until you find those you like. There are a number of options for pattern work, such as Swedish Tracing Paper (an interfacing-like product), tissue paper, architect's trace, alpha-numeric grid paper used in the industry, and exam table paper. The advantage of using paper instead of an interfacing-type product or taking apart a muslin and using the fabric itself for a pattern is that paper is exact and cannot stretch out of shape.

Transparent straight edge rulers (1) allow you to view the pattern while drafting. See-through rulers marked in ⅛" (3 mm) increments are particularly handy and are available in several lengths.

Fashion ruler/styling design rulers (2) provide excellent curvature for pattern adjustments and pattern drafting.

French curves (3) provide additional curvatures; they are nice to have but not essential.

Right-angle rulers (4) are also convenient and can be triangles, L-squares, or T-squares.

Measuring tape (5) that does not stretch, either reinforced fiberglass or waterproof oilcloth.

Yardstick (6) for checking fitting axis during the fitting process.

Pencils (7) that make a precise, easy-to-read line and are comfortable in your hand. Mechanical pencils don't need sharpening.

Colored pencils (8) are particularly handy when making multiple pattern adjustments and you want to indicate which line to use; they're also helpful for drawing axis lines on a fitting muslin.

Fabric eraser (9) can be used to remove light pencil marks without abrading or marking the fabric.

Pencil sharpener (10) for wooden and colored pencils.

Fine-tip markers (11) for marking pinned adjustments on a muslin.

Pattern paper of your choice (12), for example architect's trace, alpha-numeric pattern paper, exam table paper. Tissue paper designed for gifts tears easily and is not recommended.

Paper scissors (13) should be comfortable in your hand and allow you to cut accurately.

Small fabric scissors (14) are helpful when clipping fitting muslin during the fitting.

Tracing wheel (15) and carbon paper if you like to transfer pattern markings to the muslin this way.

Clear tape (16) for adding paper to patterns and making pattern adjustments. Some are more flexible than others, some are removable. I prefer ½" (1.3 cm) Magic tape in a desk dispenser.

Colored tape (not shown) for marking the yardstick; blue painter's masking tape is easy to remove and leaves no adhesive residue.

Table or work area (17) large enough to spread your pattern out. An elevated table prevents back strain. A clean kitchen counter works well. You can easily elevate a table with bed lifts or PVC pipe (that the table legs can slip into) cut to the appropriate length.

Muslin (18) or other stable fabric for test garments. Woven gingham is often off-grain, and so is not actually helpful. Some people like pattern tracing fabric or lightweight nonwoven interfacing, so the pattern itself can be used as a test-fitting garment; while convenient, this method is not as accurate as keeping a separate paper pattern.

Pins (19) for fitting the muslin should be sharp and easy to use. I prefer glass head pins. Some people find a wrist pincushion convenient.

Elastic (20), ¼" to ⅜" (6 to 10 mm) wide, for anchoring skirts and pants during a fitting, and assisting in taking waist measurements.

Sewing machine and basic sewing notions (not shown) for making test-fitting garments.

Iron and ironing board (not shown) for pressing test fabric, constructing test garments, and pressing fitted muslin pieces flat.

Full-length mirror (not shown) for fitting test garments. Having an additional mirror allows you to easily see your back and sides without turning the body and distorting the test garment.

Dress form (not shown) made or padded to measurements is convenient but not necessary. Fitting test garments on the body is better for getting accurate proportions.

the fitting process

THE INTERRELATIONSHIP BETWEEN PATTERNS AND FITTING

To get a pattern to fit, use the pattern in conjunction with a test garment (or fitting muslin). The fitting muslin is your laboratory, where you can experiment with changes so the fit is good and the garment's proportions are flattering. The pattern is the record-keeping device where you make the fitting changes so that you can reproduce the garment.

Understanding the principles of flat pattern manipulation helps you become a more effective fitter. For example, you will know to make changes on the fitting muslin in such a way that they can later be made in the pattern. Understanding the principles of fitting advances your ability to alter and adjust patterns. For instance, you will be more aware of how a change to one pattern piece affects an adjacent pattern piece.

The two skills of fitting and patternmaking support one another in many ways. When you are fitting, you will know that you can fine-tune the subtlety of a curve with your ruler on the pattern. When you are adjusting a pattern, you will be guided by both the visual and tactile knowledge you have of the individual's body. Strengthening one skill leads to the enhancement of the other skill.

OVERVIEW OF THE FITTING PROCESS

Getting a pattern to fit is a process. Sometimes it's a simple and short process, and other times it's long and involved. Some garment styles are more straightforward to fit than others, and some individuals are easier to fit than others. But the general process is always the same. The following chapters describe the process in detail.

1 Make preliminary adjustments to the pattern, if desired.

2 Mark and sew a test garment.

3 Fit the test garment. This requires training the eye to recognize fitting issues, deciding which fitting changes to make first, and knowing when to stop a fitting.

4 Mark the changes pinned on the test garment and remove the pins.

5 Transfer the markings on the test garment to the pattern.

6 Alter and manipulate the pattern. This requires learning basic pattern manipulation techniques.

7 True the pattern (that is, check that adjacent seams on the pattern are the same length).

8 Mark and sew another test garment, repeating the process until the fit and the pattern are perfected.

FRESH STARTS

Rather than trying to fit the entire test garment in one session, it can be helpful to stop a fitting after you pin a small number of changes. Making those changes on the pattern and sewing a new test garment often makes it easy to see which fitting changes to make next. Plus, you can double-check that what you've done so far is indeed improving the fit. If a large number of fitting changes are made in a single session and a new fitting issue is introduced, it can be quite difficult to assess what caused the new problem.

recognizing fitting issues

Training the eye to recognize fitting issues requires time. Masters at fitting have studied and practiced for years, and they have fit hundreds of garments on all types of bodies. Once you can recognize a few fitting issues, you'll be able to concentrate on others, gradually building a comprehensive understanding of fitting. Fitting is a skill that can be learned, but you may need to train your eye to see fabric in new ways.

DRAG LINES

Drag lines are diagonal or horizontal pulls in the fabric. They usually radiate from the point where the problem originates; however, since there is a beginning and endpoint to the drag line, determining which is the origination point can be confusing. Drag lines indicate that a garment is too tight or that there is not enough three-dimensional space for a mound of flesh. They can occur on any type of garment.

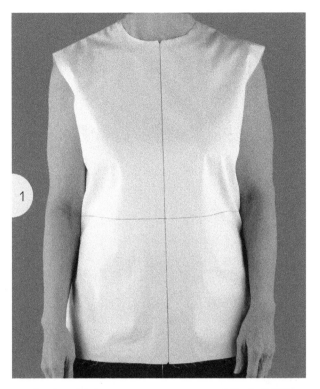

1 The diagonal pulls in the fabric starting at the bust and going to the side below the horizontal balance line (HBL) are typical drag lines. They originate at the bust, indicating that there is a fitting issue involving the bust.

2 Although there are a number of fitting issues in the shoulder area, the diagonal folds of fabric running from the bust to the side seam near the waist are drag lines that indicate the need for more bust shaping. The horizontal pulls in the fabric at bust level across the center front of the garment also indicate that the garment is too tight across the bust.

FABRIC FLARING AWAY FROM THE BODY

Except for designs where the fabric is intended to flare, fabric flaring away from the body signals a fitting problem. It usually indicates that the HBL is not level.

SMALL DRAG LINES FROM PINS

Pins often create very small drag lines of their own. This is due to the path of the pin in the cloth, where the fabric is being pushed in one direction and then pulled back down in the opposite direction.

1 The front of this garment flares away from the body at the hemline. This suggests that the HBL is not level. In this example, the drag lines emanating from the bust indicate that more bust shaping is necessary.

2 With practice, your eye will quickly learn to disregard the small aberrations in the cloth created by pins.

FOLDS

Folds are symptomatic of fabric excess. Vertical folds indicate too much circumference; horizontal folds indicate too much length. Folds do not always form where the problem is stemming from. For instance, if a bodice has horizontal folds at the waist, there could be too much length in the upper torso between the underarm and the shoulder, or in the lower torso between the underarm and the waist.

1 The vertical folds of fabric at the sides from the mid-back through the waist indicate that there is too much circumference in this garment back.

2 The horizontal fold of fabric across the mid-back indicates that there is too much length in the bodice above the waist.

3 Here is the same garment viewed from the back.

PRACTICE SEEING FITTING ISSUES

Any time you're around people, whether it's at the office or the grocery store, look at the fit of the clothes people are wearing. Does a blouse have a drag line radiating from the bust toward the hip? Does a jacket ride up on the buttock? Is a skirt hemline shorter in the back than the front? The power of observation—our ability to see and understand what we are seeing—grows with practice.

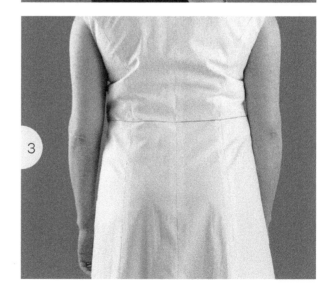

glossary of patternmaking terms

Apex: The furthest protruding point of the bust.

Blending a seam: Redrawing a seam to eliminate jogs or angles by making a smooth and continuous line.

Bust point: See "apex."

Close-wedge: A manipulation used to shorten a fitting muslin or a pattern by an uneven amount.

Cut line: The line indicating where to cut the pattern.

Dart intake: The distance between dart legs, measured at the seam line.

Dart legs: The lines on each side of a dart; the stitching lines for a dart.

Dart point: The point or dot indicating the end or termination of a dart.

Dart equivalent: The amount equal to a dart intake.

Dart extension: The area to the side of a dart that is frequently triangular in shape and protrudes further out than the rest of the pattern or garment until the dart is closed and folded in the proper direction.

Dart transfer: Moving a dart to another location.

Fine-tune: To make a small adjustment that results in further improvement.

Fold line: A line indicating that the pattern piece is to be positioned on fabric that is folded in half when cutting the garment out.

Grainline arrow: A straight line on the pattern indicating how to position the pattern piece on the fabric; the grainline arrow on the pattern is placed parallel to the selvage of the fabric.

Grid board: A flat board marked with a series of regularly spaced parallel and perpendicular lines.

Intersecting seam line: A seam that crosses or intersects another seam.

Notch: A registration mark on the pattern, often shaped as a small triangle.

Open-wedge: A manipulation used to lengthen a fitting muslin or a pattern by an uneven amount.

Seam allowance: The distance between the seam line and the cut line.

Seam line: The line on the pattern indicating where the garment is to be stitched.

Spread: A manipulation used to lengthen a fitting muslin or a pattern by an even amount.

Stacking pattern pieces: Placing adjoining pattern pieces one on top of the other, matching the seam lines and any notches. Often the top pattern piece has been folded along the seam line.

Tick mark: A short line. A series of tick marks are used to indicate an approximate seam placement, which can then be finalized and drafted permanently.

Tuck: A manipulation used to shorten a fitting muslin or a pattern by an even amount.

Truing a seam: Checking that seams on a pattern are blended nicely and that two adjoining seams are the same length or incorporate the desired amount of ease, then making any necessary corrections.

Waist-fitting dart: A vertical dart starting below the bust.

Walking a seam: The process of comparing the same seam on two adjoining pattern pieces.

Wedge: A manipulation used to shorten or lengthen a fitting muslin or pattern by an uneven amount. See "close-wedge" and "open-wedge."

CREATING A FITTING MUSLIN

Getting a pattern to fit is a process. Sometimes it's a simple and short process, and other times it's long and involved. A fitting muslin is your laboratory for that process. This chapter describes how to create and mark a test garment (or fitting muslin), how certain markings help with the fitting process, and many other fitting muslin fundamentals.

a framework for fitting

Making fitting adjustments without a framework to work within relies on a lot of luck. Sometimes you'll make progress, and sometimes you won't. And when a fitting adjustment does work, you frequently won't understand why it did so—although you'll probably feel very grateful that it did. Using a fitting axis, described below, establishes a framework you can work in. This, in turn, allows you to conduct the fitting methodically. At each step, you'll know what you're trying to achieve, even if you have to figure out how to achieve it. The fitting axis is what puts you in control of the fitting process.

THE FITTING AXIS

A fitting axis establishes fixed lines around which the fabric is manipulated. Without such a fitting axis, correcting one fitting issue can cause a different fitting issue to develop. You're usually flying by the seat of your pants and hoping for the best. With a fitting axis, on the other hand, you approach fitting a muslin with purpose and direction.

To understand the fitting axis or framework, think of a straight skirt made with plaid fabric. Center front is a constant line that doesn't get altered, and it is the first component of the axis. It is a straight line that is perpendicular to the floor.

At the hem of the skirt, one color line of the plaid shows evenly all the way around the skirt. This line, the hemline, is parallel to the floor, and it is used to establish the second component of the fitting axis.

A

Move up the body to the hip, which is usually the fullest part of the buttock, to establish the second component of the fitting axis. Viewed from the front, the hip level is below where the body begins to taper toward the waist. The hip level, which is parallel to the hemline, is the second component of the fitting axis **(A)**.

The fitting axis allows you to develop your most important fitting tool—the horizontal balance line.

THE HORIZONTAL BALANCE LINE

The line at the hip level of the skirt is referred to as the horizontal balance line, or HBL. Due to how the HBL is derived, the HBL is always parallel to the floor and perpendicular to the center front. On a skirt, most of the fitting takes place above the HBL, as the fabric is shaped to follow the contours of the lower torso. If the fitting axis is kept in correct position, the hemline will follow one color line of the plaid fabric, and the skirt will hang straight and plumb **(A)**.

If the HBL is not employed when fitting the skirt, the fabric can be successfully shaped to follow the contours of the body. But depending on how the fitting was executed, the hemline might not follow one color line of the plaid fabric, in which case the skirt will most likely flare away from the body at either the front or the back **(B)**.

On garments that hang from the shoulder (tops, dresses, jackets, and coats), an HBL is placed between the bust and the waist. A dress is a good example of how the torso HBL is derived: it is an additional line that is parallel to the hem and to the hip-level HBL. If the garment length extends below the hip, another HBL drawn at hip level facilitates the fitting process. If the garment length ends above the hip, use the one HBL on the torso between the bust and the waist **(C)**.

A garment with a shaped hem follows the same principles, because the shaped hem is actually a stylistic element. The fitting process is often streamlined if the fitting muslin has a straight hem. Complete the fitting, and then create the hem shaping **(D)**.

CENTER BACK AXIS LINE

Center back is not as useful as center front for the perpendicular component of the fitting axis, because back seams of garments often incorporate shaping. However, when fitting the back, it can be helpful to imagine a center back axis line, especially in relation to keeping the HBL level.

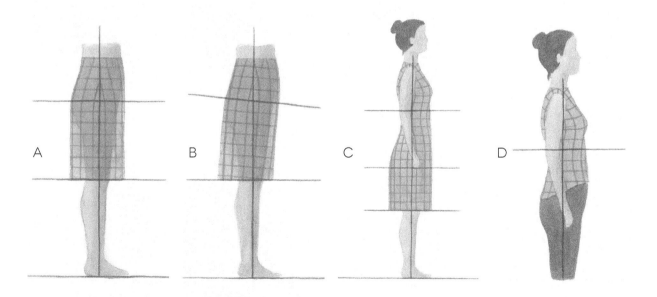

A B C D

ESTABLISHING THE HBL ON THE PATTERN

On many commercial patterns, the lengthen/shorten line can be used for the HBL. But it's also easy to establish an HBL if there are no lengthen/shorten lines, and to check that the lengthen/shorten lines on the pattern are at the same level. The following process is the same for any type of garment.

In order to establish a horizontal balance line, you must be familiar with walking patterns (see page 82). Start with the front pattern piece. The HBL is perpendicular to the center front. Because the grainline arrow is parallel to the center front, the HBL is also perpendicular to the grainline arrow. In fact, horizontal balance lines are always perpendicular to the grainline arrow on garments cut on the straight-of-grain. On bias-cut garments, the HBL is at a 45-degree angle to the straight-of-grain.

1 Place the HBL at or just below the fullest part of the hip on a skirt or pants.

2 Place the HBL between the bust and waist on a top, dress, jacket, or coat.

FITTING TIP

If it facilitates the fitting process, draw more than one HBL on the fitting muslin.

When the fitting muslin is prepared, the HBL will be drawn on the outside of the cloth so that it is easily seen. For instructions to do this, see page 42.

1 To establish the HBL on the adjacent pattern piece, walk the two pattern pieces from the hem to the HBL placement, and mark the HBL placement on the corresponding pattern piece at the seam line.

2 Place the adjacent pattern piece on a grid board, and move the grainline arrow along a vertical grid line until the match point at the seam line comes to a horizontal grid line.

3 Draw the HBL, using the horizontal grid line at the match point. Accurate work is important.

Using the HBL During a Fitting

During the fitting process, the HBL is a landmark to utilize, a concrete reference point. Learning to bring the fitting axis into position and to manipulate the fabric around the fitting axis takes practice. But luck is removed from the process and replaced with educated trial and error. With only a small amount of experience, you'll understand that fitting is simply a matter of manipulating the fabric around the fitting axis so that it creates the space required by a body's unique shape.

muslin essentials

LEARNING TO LOOK

Fitting a muslin requires actively looking. Most of what we see during the day is processed passively, even though we are taking in a large amount of information. When learning to fit, it's essential to think actively about what you are seeing. At first, you must learn to notice that a fitting issue exists. With experience, you'll become a discerning observer, reading the fabric in a way that reveals the cause of the fitting issue.

Using a Mirror and Photographs

Because we need to pin and manipulate the fabric during a fitting, we work with the muslin at close range. However, an alteration that takes care of a particular fitting issue in one area might not be the best solution in terms of making the client look proportionate and balanced as a whole. So periodically it's helpful to look at the muslin within a larger context.

To do this, you can step away from the individual if you are fitting someone else, or you can sight in to a full-length mirror that's several feet away. When fitting yourself, using one or more mirrors lets you view the muslin while in a normal stance.

A mirror is helpful for several reasons: Using a mirror permits us to view the subject from further away, which reduces the size of the entire image and allows us to see the specific area of interest within a larger context. Also, when looking directly at a muslin, we are viewing a three-dimensional figure. The reflection in the mirror is two-dimensional, and this dimensional change often makes it easier to identify fitting issues.

A mirror also helps us view fitting issues creatively. When we fit, we tend to latch on to the first solution that comes to mind. Sighting in a mirror to shift the context encourages us to observe in a new way. This often leads us to other potential solutions.

Using photographs to study fitting problems provides the same benefits as sighting in a mirror. When fitting oneself, a photograph may seem less personal, and this step of removal makes it easier to look at our own body more objectively. Any tool that enables you to understand what you are seeing not only helps elucidate the problem at hand, but also increases your ability to observe in general.

THE BODY AS "VOLUME"

Fitting is a complicated process. Yet, in essence, the fitting process is simply a matter of making the space created by the fitting muslin match the space occupied by the body. There is no mystique—it is just a puzzle to solve. You manipulate the muslin so that its three-dimensional space reflects the volume of the body.

In addition to matching the total volume, the muslin must also reflect where the body mass is located. For instance, two women with exactly the same full bust measurement could have quite different body proportions. One could have a broad back and small breasts, and the other could have a narrow back and large breasts. The total full bust measurement is the same, but the two patterns and fitting muslins look very different. One will have a wide back pattern, and the other a narrow back pattern. One will have less space for breast tissue, and the other more space for breast tissue.

However, the process of fitting is the same for both figures. Move the fabric of the muslin to bring the fitting axis into position, and then manipulate the fitting muslin's volume so that it reflects the body (volume) you are fitting.

FITTING OTHERS AND YOURSELF

Conducting a fitting on another person has many advantages. You can walk around the individual, viewing the muslin from all different vantage points. You can study the muslin itself as well as the reflected image in the mirror. Your hands can work independently or together. And you have easy access to all parts of the muslin.

Having a fitting buddy is a productive approach for many sewers. You have the advantages of fitting another person, plus another set of discerning eyes. Especially when you are learning to fit, one person might detect issues that the other doesn't happen to see. And you can problem solve the fitting issues together.

Weight Fluctuation

Some women have almost no variation in their weight, whereas other women experience a good deal of weight fluctuation. A few pounds of weight gain or loss can affect the way a garment fits. With some clients, I feel like I'm trying to fit a moving target from one fitting session to the next. For someone whose weight fluctuates, it's important not to overfit the test muslin and realize that, as the fitter, you might have a very difficult time getting an absolutely perfect fit.

Fitting Yourself

Fitting yourself is possible, but it requires patience. The limitations of not being able to see or touch every part of the muslin are the biggest obstacles. Setting up an extra mirror or two helps you see your sides and back.

Pinning changes to the muslin is especially difficult. On the front, try using your dominant hand to pin changes on the other side of the body. This also works for making most changes to the side of the garment. For the back, be prepared to take off and put on your garment a number of times.

Identifying fitting issues and imagining the pinned solution are valuable assets. Visualize the change that needs to be made, remove the garment, manipulate and pin the fabric, then put the garment back on. When assessing the results, differentiate whether you need to fine-tune the pinned correction, move the location of the adjustment, or start anew.

If your frustration level rises, set the project aside for a couple of hours or days and try again. Fitting yourself is largely a matter of perseverance and determination. A bit of assistance is very helpful. For example, you can teach a non-sewer how to pin. Then, using your ability to observe and assess the muslin, instruct your "helping hands" where to do the pinning.

Fitting Another Person

Fitting a muslin on someone else requires touching that person. An experienced fitter knows that the first task is to build trust between herself and the individual she's fitting. This will allow the person who's being fitted to relax, enabling the fitter to do her job. The approach I've developed with my clients will help guide the interaction between you and your fitting buddy.

To build trust, I have my client put on the fitting muslin, and I pin it closed. I then stand behind her while she faces the mirror. As I make my first visual assessment of the muslin, I lightly touch her upper back. I then walk around her and perhaps gently touch her shoulder. While she is becoming accustomed to my hand on her body, I'm becoming familiar with how the muslin fits.

If my client seems comfortable, I can start the fitting in earnest. If she doesn't, I talk about what I'm observing. For example, "This fold of fabric indicates that we need to increase the bust dart. I'll show you the difference." This provides a good transition to pinning one or two changes. At the next session, the client is likely to be more at ease because she already knows what a fitting session entails. Plus, when she sees that the new muslin fits better, her confidence in the process and trust in you grows.

Touching my client's body gives me additional information that my eyes alone cannot pick up. After a fitting has been completed, I'll have a sense of the client's body in my hands. This information "in my fingers" helps me tremendously as I use the fashion ruler to make the changes on the pattern.

FITTING TIP

Standing in one place for more than five or ten minutes is tiring, so be sure to have your client periodically move around and do a few knee bends.

Comfort: One Indication of Good Fit

It's important to get feedback about how the muslin feels on the wearer's body. If you are fitting yourself, you'll need to play the role of both the fitter and the client.

Sometimes a client will voluntarily say that something feels much better after you correct a fitting issue. If the client does not spontaneously provide feedback, you'll need to ask (for example, "Does the armhole feel better now that I've clipped it?"). If you notice that an area of the garment is close fitting, ask the client how it feels (for example, "Does the bodice feel tight across the bust?"). Her comments are important clues as to how the fitting is proceeding, and they often reveal areas that need your attention as a fitter.

The ultimate goal is to have the client feel comfortable and relaxed in her garment. We all have quirks about what feels comfortable and what doesn't. Some people can't stand to have a tight sleeve; others don't like looseness across the bust. These are very real issues to the person being fit, even if you don't personally share these likes and dislikes.

Experimentation is part of the process. You might need to try several different things to achieve both comfort and good fit. In addition to asking yourself which change makes the garment look better, ask the client which feels better.

Take Your Time

Many people do not know what good fit is and have never owned a garment that fits properly. Taking small steps toward getting the garment to fit correctly is the best approach. Rather than trying to make all of the fitting changes in one session, make the most important changes first. Correct the pattern and make a new test garment. During the next fitting session, make a few more changes.

In this way, you make the fitting process easier on yourself as the fitter, and you will gradually lead the client to understand what good fit is. This strategy also works well if you are fitting yourself: as the fit slowly improves, you more readily will see what needs to be done next.

WHAT TO WEAR FOR A FITTING

Because foundation garments, layering garments, and shoes affect the way a garment fits, they must be taken into account during the development of a muslin.

Foundation Garments

Wear whatever undergarments you normally would wear under the garment being developed. Undergarments should fit properly; for example, a worn-out bra lowers the bustline, and too-tight panties create a bulge above and below the elastic band.

Layering Garments

When fitting a muslin such as a jacket, wear what you normally would wear under the finished jacket, perhaps a camisole, blouse, or sweater. I suggest to my clients that they wear the bulkiest potential layering garment during the fitting process. If a variety of garments will be worn under the finished jacket, the fit will likely be compromised at one end of the spectrum. For instance, if the finished jacket was fit to accommodate a sweater, it will probably look a bit loose with only a camisole. Deciding on the range of layering garments is simply a choice that the wearer must make.

Once you have a pattern that fits well, you can turn it into a bigger or smaller garment with a handful of pattern changes. For instance, if you have a shoulder princess blouse, you can scale it up to make a shoulder princess jacket or even a shoulder princess coat. You can also scale the garment down, turning a jacket into a blouse. For information on how to do this, see page 100.

Shoes

Wear the shoes that you intend to wear with the garment. Heel height impacts the length of garments, especially pants. But heel height also changes your stance, which in turn affects the fit. There might not be much difference at all between a 1" and a 1½" (2.5 and 3.8 cm) heel, but there will be a more noticeable difference between a 1" and a 2½" (2.5 and 6.4 cm) heel, and a sizeable difference between a 1" and a 4" (2.5 and 10.2 cm) heel. If you don't have shoes picked out for the garment, choose a shoe with a heel height that's close to what you envision wearing.

preparing a muslin

CHOOSING FABRIC FOR A TEST GARMENT

For garments that will be made from a woven fabric, choose a stable woven fabric for the test garment. If the fashion fabric that will be used contains spandex, select a fabric for the test garment that has a similar amount of spandex. However, if the fashion fabric that will be used is drapey, I recommend using a stable (non-drapey) fabric for at least the first and perhaps the second test garment; this will ensure that you don't rely on the drape of the fabric to solve fitting issues. If the fashion fabric that will be used is thick, such as for a coat, it's helpful to use a similarly thick fabric for the test garment.

For garments that will be made from knit fabric, choose a knit for the test garment that has similar give and stretch qualities in the length-of-grain and the cross grain.

I prefer a light-colored fabric, which is easier to "read" (detect fitting issues) than a dark-colored fabric. With a light-colored fabric, it's also easier to see the markings transferred from the pattern and to make notations during the fitting.

Muslin fabric is often used—which is why a test garment is also referred to as "a muslin." Muslin fabric varies in weight and quality. With experimentation, you'll find test fabrics that you like to work with and that suit your budget. I like to keep a good supply of test garment fabric on hand, since I know I'll be making several different test muslins in the process of getting a pattern to fit well.

Muslin fabric and other inexpensive fabrics are frequently off-grain. Fortunately, most muslin and many other inexpensive woven cottons are stable enough that the fabric being slightly off-grain isn't a big issue. While straightening the grain of fashion fabric before cutting out a pattern is very important because of the impact grain line has on how a garment hangs, do the best you can with test garment fabrics without driving yourself crazy.

I do not preshrink my test garment fabric because I like the extra stability provided by the small amount of sizing in muslin and other inexpensive cottons.

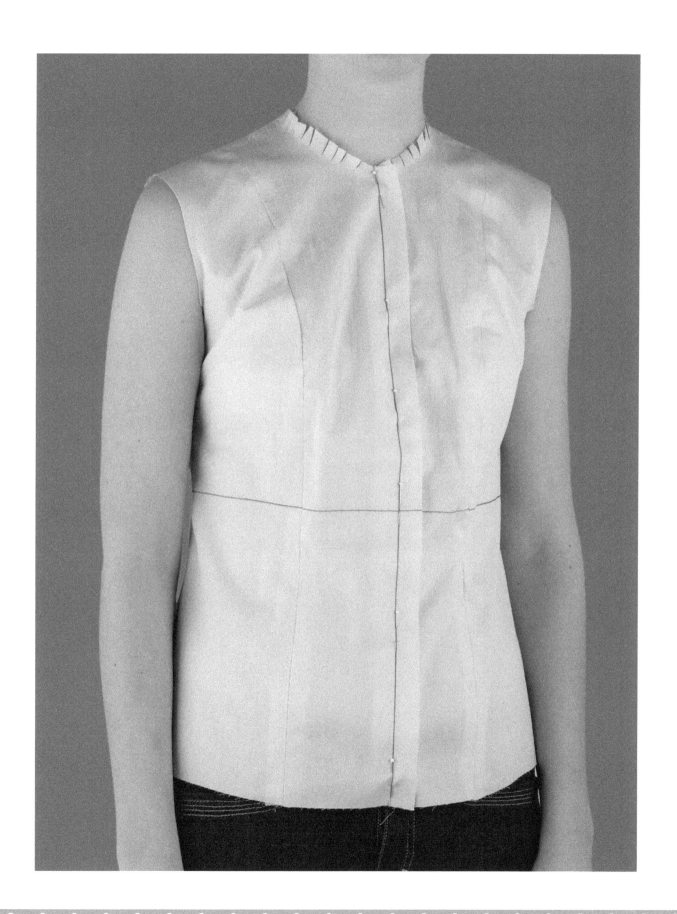

CUTTING OUT AND MARKING THE TEST MUSLIN

I cut out most test muslins by placing the pattern on fabric that has been folded in half, so that I cut a right and a left side of the garment at the same time. Making test garments as efficiently as possible without sacrificing accuracy helps speed up the entire process.

Marking the test muslin with pertinent information from the pattern facilitates the fitting process. With experience, you'll learn what information is helpful to you and what is extraneous. And with experimentation, you'll also figure out the method you like to use to transfer this information.

Information to Transfer

The landmarks listed below should be transferred from the pattern to the right side of the muslin. Some fitters also like to mark the bust apex, grainlines, seam lines, hemlines, notches, and match points.

Center front. This is one of the axis lines and therefore it should be noted on the fitting muslin. For a garment with an asymmetric front, having center front marked provides a visual reference.

Garment opening. Mark the seam lines of the garment opening so that you accurately pin the fitting muslin closed. On garments with a center front opening, the center fronts are the match lines; having them marked is important since the amount of fabric between the center front and the cut edge will vary depending on the size of button or other type of closure. For asymmetric garments, mark the match lines, which might also be center front.

Horizontal balance line. Make sure that the HBL is easy to see, since it is a very important fitting tool. Mark more than one HBL on the fitting muslin if it would be helpful. For example, on a sheath dress, I would mark one HBL between the bust and the waist, and another HBL at or just below the full hip. See page 32 for how to mark a HBL on the pattern.

Darts. Mark all darts on the muslin, whether or not you sew them before conducting a fitting. On first muslins, I don't sew waist darts on skirts and pants because I prefer to drape them in as I assess the client's body. However, having them drawn on the muslin provides a convenient frame of reference in fitting the right and left side symmetrically. Even though I sew bust darts and shoulder darts prior to fitting, having the dart legs drawn on the muslin is helpful if I need to reposition them during the fitting.

HOW TO TRANSFER THE MARKINGS

I use both dressmaker's carbon and colored pencil. I rarely thread trace the pattern markings because of the risk of the threads coming out of the fabric during the fitting process, and because I can't see the thread tracing as easily. Mark the test muslin after it's been cut out, but before removing all the pins holding the pattern to the fabric.

Using Dressmaker's Carbon or Transfer Paper

1 Insert two layers of carbon paper between the layers of fabric, with the carbon facing each layer of fabric.

2 Using a tracing wheel, go over the lines or symbols on the pattern to be transferred.

3 An accurately marked dart.

TEST GARMENT OPENINGS

Decide where you want the garment access (opening) to be on the fitting muslin. It is often helpful to have the opening in a different location than where it will be on the finished garment. For instance, I prefer a center back opening when fitting pants, which eliminates the bulk of a front fly and allows me to see the fit of the front crotch curve more easily.

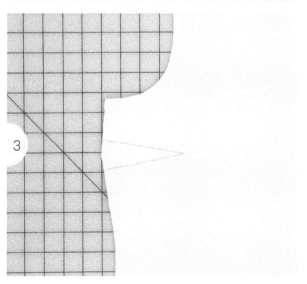

Marking Horizontal Balance Lines and Center Fronts

To get very accurate, straight lines, I mark horizontal balance lines and center fronts with the method described below:

1 Make a small clip at the HBL. In this example, the bodice back pattern piece has a seam at center back, so the HBL is clipped along both the center back seam and the side seam.

2 Open the fabric, align a ruler with the clips, and draw the HBL. Repeat for the other back piece.

3 The accurately marked HBL.

SEWING THE TEST MUSLIN

Use a long stitch length when constructing the test garment so that it is easy to release a seam or dart during the fitting process. Check that the lengthened stitch does not, however, produce a puckered seam.

Press the seam allowances and darts as you would for a real garment. I prefer to have the seam allowances against the body. Some people like to fit with the seam allowances on the outside of the garment because it's easier to adjust and pin the seams. While this is true, I find the seam allowances very distracting when reading the fabric for fitting issues and when assessing how the finished lines of the garment look on the body. If the muslin is simply turned inside out in order to put the seam allowances on the outside of the test garment, it can also lead to confusion if the client's body is uneven (for example, has one high shoulder), because the left side of the test muslin would be on the right side of the body.

Stay stitching seam lines is not necessary except in areas where the fabric would stretch out of shape very easily. If my test garment fabric is quite stable, I stay stitch seam lines such as the waist or neck only when I am working on a final muslin. When stay stitching, use a regular stitch length (ten to twelve stitches per inch [2.5 cm]), and check that the stitching is not causing the fabric to pucker.

Do not put zippers in initial fitting muslins, because they make it very difficult to pin some fitting adjustments, such as shortening a garment. It's fine to put a zipper in a final muslin. If you are fitting yourself and have a garment with a back closure, feel free to change the placement of the opening for the purpose of fitting the muslin so it's easy to get in and out of the garment by yourself.

Sew together the basic garment sections but omit stylistic elements and details. For instance, do not conduct initial fittings with collars, because a neckline that reflects the client's body must first be established. Do not conduct initial fittings with sleeves sewn into the garment, because a sleeve can distort the fit of the rest of the garment. Distill the garment down to its most basic pattern elements, and this is where you want to start the fitting process.

After constructing the test garment, give it a final press so that the fabric is not wrinkled. Do not starch the fabric, however, as this might prevent the fabric from relaxing on the client's body.

adjusting a muslin

CLIPPING AND MARKING DURING A FITTING

Tightness in a test garment distorts the fit. The first step in the fitting process is to release seams and clip garment areas that are tight. This allows the garment to relax on the body, which is essential before proceeding with the fitting. Periodically during the fitting process, check the test garment again for signs of tightness.

Alleviating Tightness at the Perimeter

Horizontal or diagonal pull lines in the fabric can—but don't always—indicate tightness. As is often the case when fitting, it's important to "read" the fabric. If you suspect tightness at the perimeter of a garment, for instance at the neckline or armhole, it's easy to check. Make several ⅜" (1 cm) clips in the seam allowance. If the fabric spreads apart between the clips, the fabric is telling you there is tightness. If the fabric does not spread apart, tightness is not the cause of the pull lines.

Gradually making the clips deeper and increasing the number of clips is a safe way to proceed. When the clips no longer spread apart or when the original pull lines in the test garment disappear, you have clipped enough.

1 This neckline is too tight, indicated by the slight strain lines between the bust and the neck. If you slipped a finger under the front neckline, you would also feel the tension against your skin. Sometimes a client will give you feedback. A neckline or waistline that is too tight will often cause the test garment to creep upward as the too-tight area seeks a smaller circumference on the body.

2 The test garment can relax on the body once the perimeter is clipped. Sometimes the clips will be within the seam allowance, but often you will need to clip beyond the seam allowance further into the garment fabric.

3 This armhole is too tight, causing slight distortion at the underarm, indicated by the small fold of fabric at the back armhole and the crumpling of fabric below the armhole. Sometimes the distortion of fabric is very noticeable, as seen on page 112.

4 Clipping the armhole allows the fabric to relax. In this example, the armhole seam was clipped well beyond the original seam line. The back armhole and sometimes the front armhole are typical places where this situation occurs.

Alleviating Tightness on the Interior

Tightness can also occur in the middle of the garment. In these instances, you must release seams in order to alleviate the tightness, since the tightness does not occur at the perimeter of the garment. Occasionally, an area of the garment that seems to be tight in the first assessment of the test muslin will no longer be tight once the proper fitting change is made. For example, if the bustline is too tight, the back of the garment might also look tight; but when adequate room for the bust is provided, the back no longer shows sign of strain.

Another example is when the back hemline of a bodice is tight across the buttocks when the HBL is lower in the back than in the front. Bringing the HBL to a level position often alleviates the tightness across the back hip. However, if you don't initially notice that the uneven HBL is the cause of the tightness at the back hip, no harm is done. Your fitting order will follow a different path. For instance, you would probably release the side seams to alleviate the tightness across the buttocks. Through the course of the fitting, you would eventually notice that the HBL was low in the back. Correcting that would likely let the side seams close up again. In this example, you would have gone through some extra steps, but the end results would be the same.

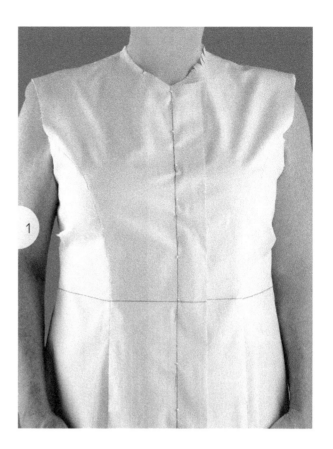

1 This bustline is too tight, indicated by the drag lines forming from the bust toward the center front at bust level.

2 Although it is not as obvious as in the previous example, this bustline is also too tight, indicated by the slight strain on the fabric at the center front where it is pinned at bust level.

3 Releasing the princess seams over the bust allows the test garment to relax on the body. Be sure to work on both sides of the body, in this case releasing the princess seam on the right front as well as the left front.

MARKING A MUSLIN DURING A FITTING

I frequently draw on my test garments while I'm conducting a fitting. To indicate the placement of a seam, draw the seam line, not the cut line. Fitting and pattern work hold this in common: always think and mark seam line.

Occasionally I'll draw a seam line on a test garment that's not quite where I want it. If this happens, two hatch marks mean "no," as is the case with pattern work.

Making notes directly on the muslin means the notes can't get lost, and they'll be right there when you're transferring the fitting changes to the pattern. As your fitting skills become more adept, you can also use notes to speed up the fitting process, although this isn't as precise as actually making the adjustment on the muslin.

1 The seam lines of the armholes and neckline have been marked as well as a new placement for the shoulder seam.

2 To determine the placement of the seam line, several tools can be used. A narrow piece of cording or soutache braid gives you something to sight on, and it's easy to move. You can also use a row of pins to mark a tentative seam line, but they aren't as fast to reposition. In some instances, such as with a shoulder line, sighting along a pencil works.

3 Two short lines or hatch marks indicate that the line should be disregarded.

4 These notations indicate that the skirt is to be let out from the mark above the HBL to the bottom of the skirt. In the pattern work, I would know to add the amount indicated down the side seam and then blend the new side seam to the upper portion of the hip curve.

PINNING

Pinning changes on a test garment so that you don't accidentally poke the wearer takes some practice. Sometimes you can place your free hand up under the garment, but most of the time you cannot without distorting the fabric. Developing a pinning technique facilitates the fitting process.

Developing a Pinning Technique

I often reposition one of the seam allowances so that both are pointing in one direction in the area of the adjustment, and then proceed as follows. First, gently push the point of the pin through the top layer of fabric only. Next, rather than pushing the pin completely through the bottom layer of fabric, which is when you might poke the client, pin into just the uppermost fibers of the bottom layer. As you do this, use the pin to gently pull the fabric of the bottom layer slightly away from the client's body. Then guide the pin a bit further into the bottom layer of fabric. Finish by arcing the pin and coming back through the top layer of fabric.

General Pinning Practices

* Pin the alteration where the fitting issue occurs. This often means you will be pinning into the middle of the garment, rather than at or along a seam.

* Pin the fitting change so that it flatters the figure. Sometimes there's a trade-off between obtaining the most effective fit and the most flattering fit.

* Pin the fitting change on the muslin in a way that the adjustment can be made on the pattern. For example, when increasing the bust shaping on a princess seam, pin the close-wedge to the opposing seam (**A**), *not* partway across the side princess panel (**B**).

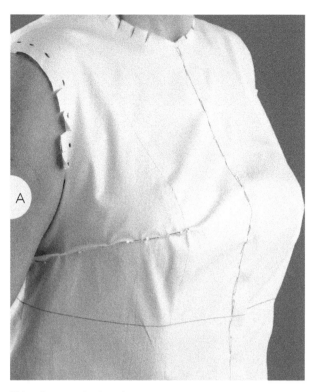

This adjustment is pinned correctly.

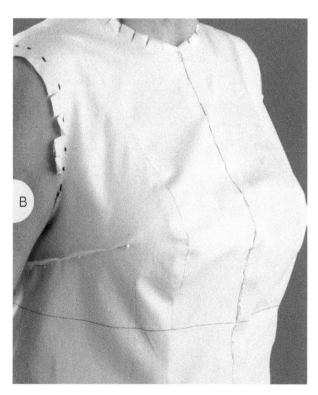

This pinning adjustment is incomplete and actually indicates the need to create a dart rather than make a close-wedge adjustment.

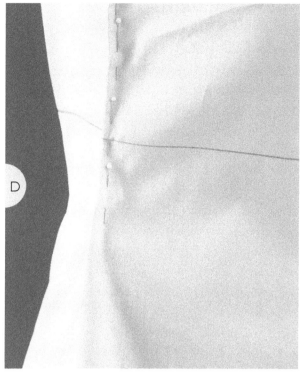

This pinning adjustment is incomplete.

This adjustment is pinned correctly.

The excess fabric on this seam has been pinned out on only one side of the seam.

The excess fabric on this seam has been pinned out equally on both seams.

* When pinning, resolve the endpoint. For example, when pinning out ¼" (6 mm) excess on a side seam, don't leave the uppermost or lowest pin with the ¼" (6 mm) intake (**C**). Rather, pin so the adjustment is blended back to the seam line (**D**).

* Pin seam adjustments so it's clear whether just one (**E**) or both sides (**F**) of the seam are affected.

* Be a considerate fitter when placing pins. Even if the pin won't poke the client, it feels threatening when the point of the pin is at the edge of the fabric and close to the skin. Place the pin so the head of its pin is nearest the garment edge.

KEEPING THE MUSLIN BALANCED

There is no such thing as a perfectly symmetrical body. Everyone has differences on one side of the body in comparison to the other. For example, the dominant arm might be larger, one shoulder might be lower, one hip might be higher, or one leg might be shorter.

Fitting the muslin very precisely on each side of the body will result in a finished garment that actually accentuates the unevenness of the figure. Rather than emphasizing the differences between the two sides of a person's body, it's preferable to fit the garment in a way that makes the body look balanced and symmetrical. Many beginners have a tendency to fit too closely, which is referred to as "overfitting." However, for most women, a balanced garment is what shows her figure to its best advantage.

When the test muslin is balanced, the pattern can also be balanced. This means there is need for only a half pattern, as is the norm for commercial patterns unless the garment is an asymmetric style.

Some women have figure variations that necessitate fitting each side of the body separately. For instance, scoliosis can cause so much curvature in the spine that the two sides of the body are quite different. In this case, each side of the body must be fit individually and a complete pattern developed. For example, a complete skirt pattern would consist of a right back and a left back, and a full front pattern that was not on the fold. When fitting unbalanced figures, the challenge is to obtain an effective fit that makes the body look as symmetrical as possible.

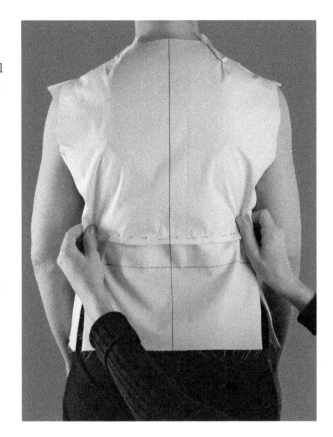

EVEN FITTING

* For a high/low shoulder, I place a shoulder pad on the low side to even out the body; the thickness of the shoulder pad should equal the amount the shoulder is low.

* To avoid overfitting, fit the high or larger side: fit the high shoulder or hip, and fit the larger arm or hip.

FITTING ORDER

Fitting is rarely a linear process that proceeds in a specified and unvarying order. There is usually a lot of going back and forth between different areas of the body. In part this happens because the test garment is not a stationary item, but it settles on the body as the fitting issues are addressed. And at the beginning of the fitting process, each time the test garment settles and relaxes on the body, it fits somewhat differently.

The fitting order also varies because you might not notice every fitting issue at the beginning of the fitting session. In addition, you must familiarize yourself with your fitting buddy's figure as well as how the fabric is lying on the body. And because of the variations in patterns, you may need to work with the fitting muslin a bit to understand the peculiarities of the pattern used for the test garment.

All of these variables contribute to the complexity of the fitting process. However, the following steps provide a general, easy-to-follow fitting order.

1 Release any area of the test garment that is tight.

2 Make the HBL level. If you aren't sure how to accomplish this, make a temporary adjustment until you can figure out the best solution. Having the fitting axis in place will help you identify and assess the fitting issues in the garment.

3 Correct any length issues, elongating or shortening the fitting muslin as needed.

4 Fit the mounds or fleshy areas of the body.

5 Revisit the HBL and fitting axis.

6 Stop anytime you feel that a new muslin reflecting the changes you've made will be helpful.

FITTING TIPS

* The fitting axis is one of the most important tools you have. Manipulate the fabric of the test garment to bring the fitting axis into correct placement. Then, within each quadrant formed by the fitting axis, manipulate the fabric to eliminate drag lines, fold lines, tightness, and excess fabric.

* Periodically during the fitting session, check the placement of landmarks such as center front, the HBL, and side seams.

* If a test muslin keeps shifting from front to back or from side to side, this usually indicates that one or more fitting issues have not been addressed and are preventing the garment from settling on the body.

* If a test muslin creeps upward on the body, this might indicate that the garment is tight. It also might be due to the garment(s) worn under the test garment. For instance, if your fitting buddy is wearing a cotton knit top that is tucked in at the waist, a skirt muslin tends to creep upward.

* Darts create three-dimensional space. Therefore, they should point to a mound or fleshy area, not to a flat or hollow area of the body.

* How large a dart is (the dart intake) affects how much three-dimensional space is created. A larger dart intake creates more three-dimensional space than a smaller dart intake.

* There is frequently more than one way to solve a particular fitting issue. Trying several options and assessing the results of each one is the best way to determine the most effective solution.

SEAMS

* The center front seam is fixed; only in rare instances is it curved.

* Side seams should hang straight and plumb.

* Center back seams can be straight or curved.

* Don't spend a lot of time fine-tuning the exact shape of every seam during a fitting. Much of this will be taken care of when the fitting changes are transferred to the pattern and the pattern work is done.

* Don't make too many changes at once. Make the most obvious changes—those you are sure about—and then make the pattern changes and a new test garment. The extra step of making a new test muslin is often a time-saver in the long run. If lots of changes are made at one time and a fitting problem is introduced or worsened, it's very difficult to determine which change caused the problem.

* Fit bodices without collars, sleeves, or other details. These additional elements can mask basic fitting problems.

* Finalize the fit of a bodice before fitting a set-in sleeve. Part of the comfort of the sleeve depends on the fit of the bodice. First get the sleeve to fit the arm; then deal with the relationship between the armhole and the sleeve cap.

* Fit tops and dresses that have waist seams (natural, empire, or dropped waist) by first fitting the bodice portion of the garment. Add the skirt after the bodice fits well.

ASSESSING THE FIT

Looking at a garment with a discerning eye is essential for a fitter. There are obvious things to check at the end of a fitting session: the HBL should be level, the side seams should be straight and plumb, there should be no signs of strain or tightness, and there should be no drag lines. But it's often difficult to assess a test garment after a number of adjustments have been made and it's full of pins, especially since the pins themselves can cause very small drag lines and dips in the fabric. This is when it's helpful to transfer the fitting changes made on the fitting muslin to the paper pattern, adjust the pattern, and make a clean test garment.

Making a second or third muslin lets you see how the adjustments have translated to the pattern and gives you the opportunity to fine-tune these changes. With a few of the most obvious fitting issues solved, a new muslin also makes it easier to identify the remaining problems.

Looking at a photograph of the fitting muslin on the body often makes it easier to identify fitting issues, as discussed on page 34. Or ask a sewing buddy for help in assessing the fit. Someone who has not been involved in the initial fitting process can frequently see fitting issues that you are missing. And talking about what you are both seeing often leads to a better understanding of what is going on and how to solve it.

In addition to a visual assessment of the fit, it's also important to assess how comfortable the garment is. Areas that are uncomfortable frequently mean that there is an underlying fitting problem.

The Benefits of Multiple Muslins

For most garments, I expect to make at least two or three fitting muslins, perhaps even more for difficult-to-fit figures. Some garments, like pants, are also more difficult to fit, so more muslins will be in order.

I don't think of making multiple muslins as "extra work." The time I put into getting a good fit is what allows me to feel relaxed when I'm ready to cut into the fashion fabric. Not only am I confident that the garment will fit nicely, but I've also become familiar with how the main portions of the garment are constructed. This results in very few, if any, unexpected problems when constructing the garment in fashion fabric.

Wearable Mock-ups

When I feel that the fit of a garment is in good shape, I often make a wearable mock-up. This is a garment made of less expensive fashion fabric that is similar in hand and weight to the "real" fashion fabric.

A wearable mock-up provides another level of checking the fit. It gives you the chance to wear the garment and go about normal activities. This often brings to light issues that were not noticed when you were just standing in front of the mirror. And if fitting issues are discovered, you've not ruined costly or irreplaceable fabric. If the fit is good, then you have another garment to wear.

Special-occasion garments do not lend themselves to making a wearable mock-up as readily as day-to-day clothing. However, sometimes you can make a slight modification; for instance, a floor-length column gown could be made as a street-length sheath dress using a less glamorous fabric.

IS IT GOOD ENOUGH?

Deciding when to stop making muslins is an important part of the fitting process. As your eye becomes better trained, you'll tend to see very small fitting issues, and it's easy to get mired in making muslins and never sew an actual garment. Sometimes "good enough" means that you're ready to make a garment, whereas with other garments, you'll decide to strive for perfection.

ALTERING PATTERNS

With basic patternmaking skills, you can make almost any pattern change. This chapter describes basic patternmaking techniques. More specialized techniques are discussed as they arise in conjunction with the fitting examples.

making flat pattern adjustments

Altering patterns can seem daunting. It's easy to feel confused or overwhelmed when you have a lot of changes to make, especially if you don't see how those changes are possible with the pattern alteration method you know.

There are a number of pattern alteration methods that you may have heard of or that you currently use, including the seam method, the pivot method, the slash method, and the box method. Depending on how your mind works, some are easier to understand and execute than others. Most simplify pattern alterations so that the method is easy to use. However, simplification almost always sacrifices precision. Most methods are also based on the assumption that a commercial pattern is intrinsically correct. Having this attitude toward patterns encourages you to search for a pattern that has been designed for your body type, so that you fit into the mold of the pattern.

My approach to pattern alteration is somewhat different in that it places the wearer's body as the focal point. There is a direct correlation between the changes made to a test muslin while it's on the body and the changes one makes to the pattern. Occasionally, only a few adjustments are necessary, but usually there are quite a number of alterations. At times there are such substantial changes to the pattern that the final product is yours more than the pattern company's.

While it may seem scary to alter patterns so freely, remember that the pattern is nothing more than a tool, a convenient starting place. This freedom is what allows for the level of precision necessary to create a garment that truly fits. And what is more, with this method it doesn't really matter which pattern you start with—the end result will be a pattern that fits.

Thus, with this method of fitting and pattern making, the key to making successful pattern alterations lies in making appropriate and precise fitting adjustments to the test garment. After fitting the test garment, you directly transfer the fitting changes to the paper pattern. Then you adjust the paper pattern in much the same way as you manipulated the muslin. Undertaking pattern work in this way puts you in control of the process. Although other pattern alteration methods may seem safer because they keep the pattern more intact, they do not allow for this level of effectiveness and exactness.

Patternmaking, like many skills, has its own specialized language. For a glossary of pattern-making terms, see page 27.

TIPS FOR ADJUSTING PATTERNS

* Work methodically, carefully, and neatly.

* Make the pattern alteration where you made the adjustment on the fitting muslin. This is where the fitting issue occurs, so change it there.

* Think seam line. In your pattern work, concentrate on the placement of the seam lines, just as you do when fitting a test garment. It's easy to adjust the seam allowances after new seam lines are established.

* Draw new seam lines using an appropriately shaped ruler, rather than freehand.

* Patterns must be flat after adjustments have been made. If there are bubbles or wrinkles when the pattern is lying on the table, this indicates that the pattern manipulation has been done incorrectly.

* Make a new copy of the pattern if prior changes make it difficult to see important landmarks. This may happen along seam lines due to redrawing or fine-tuning, or in areas where there is so much tape and added paper to be bothersome.

transferring muslin markings to a pattern

First, mark the fitting changes on the muslin. Use a marker or pencil in a contrasting color so that the fitting changes are easy to see and are different from muslin markings such as dart legs and grainlines. A bright color works best. Then transfer the markings to the pattern.

1 Mark both sides of each pin used in the fitting process.

2 Take all pins out and press the muslin flat.

SIDES OF THE PATTERN

It doesn't matter which side of the pattern you work on. Sometimes during pattern work you'll work on the side with the writing, and other times you'll work on the opposite side.

3 Lay the pattern over the muslin, aligning the edges and markings such as the HBL. Taking the muslin apart often makes it easier.

4 Transfer the markings to the pattern with a series of tick marks.

5 The pattern piece with all of the fitting changes indicated by tick marks is now ready to be altered and manipulated. For beginners, transfer all of the fitting changes from the muslin to the pattern pieces before making any pattern changes.

The tick marks represent alterations that need to be made to the pattern. Some seams might have little or no change, while others have substantial changes.

For many people, making significant changes like completely redrawing a seam line feels unorthodox and risky. However, if the fitting changes you made to the muslin while it was on the body improved the fit, and if you accurately transferred the muslin changes to the pattern, then it's logical that you can trust those alterations. When approaching fit and pattern work in this way, it's not important to keep the pattern intact; rather, your goal is to make the pattern changes based on discerning fitting changes.

using rulers to adjust seams and seam allowances

BLENDING SEAM LINES

Because pinning during a fitting can be challenging and awkward, it's difficult to pin a seam smoothly and in a perfect blend. Blending seams is an important part of patternmaking, since abrupt transitions are noticeable in the garment. For most pattern alterations, long and gentle blends translate to a garment that's more flattering. Short and choppy blends produce less flattering seams.

Therefore, when you blend a seam on the pattern using the tick marks as your guide, there will be times that one or two tick marks do not fall on a well-blended line. It's more important to capture the intention of the line than it is to connect every single tick mark. As your patternmaking skills improve, you'll feel more confident interpreting the tick marks. And you'll always have the chance to fine-tune how a seam lies on the body if you make another test garment.

When part of a seam line changes, the new seam is blended to the existing seam. Many commercial patterns, especially multi-sized patterns, do not have seam lines drawn on the pattern paper. When connecting a newly drawn or altered seam to the original seam line, it's important to first draw the existing seam line on the pattern paper so you have something to blend the new line to. If you are new to pattern work, I recommend drawing all the existing seam lines on the pattern before starting to alter the pattern.

INTERSECTING SEAMS

Seams that intersect center front and center back require special attention at the point of intersection. Waistlines and necklines are good examples. Draft waist and neck seams so they are straight and perpendicular to center front or center back for approximately ⅜" (1 cm) before they begin to curve. Otherwise, there will be an unsightly dip or point in the waist or neck seam at the intersection.

WORKING WITH RULERS

Pattern work requires precision in order for the garment to fit as intended, which is why it's important to use rulers. For example, if you inadvertently added just ¹⁄₁₆" (1.6 mm) to each seam on an eight-gore skirt, the skirt would be 1" (2.5 cm) larger than desired. Another example is the curvature of the seams over the bust: an inexact line could change not only the overall size of the garment, but also the placement of the fullness over the bust, leading to an unflattering fit. Using rulers makes your pattern work exact.

A straight edge ruler and a fashion ruler (Styling Design Ruler) are the most frequently used rulers, although a hip curve and one or more French curves are also handy. With practice and experience, your rulers will become extensions of your hands. If I were shown a seam line to blend, I might not be able to verbally describe what part of the fashion ruler to use.

But when I picked up the ruler, my hands would automatically know how to orient it for an effective blend. Your eyes and hands will also learn to use the rulers adeptly—all it takes is practice.

With the fashion ruler, you are able to produce a wide variety of curved and arced lines. The subtle shaping in seam lines can greatly influence how the garment looks on the body. For example, if a woman carries weight on the outside of her upper thigh, you can accentuate or minimize her build by the way you blend the side seam from the fullest part of the thigh to the knee on a skirt or pants. As a patternmaker, you therefore have the ability to control not only the fit, but also how a viewer's eyes perceive the body.

If the blend requires slight reshaping, you usually have several options, so it's important to think about what you want to accomplish and to experiment with different ruler positions. For instance, if the intent of the alteration is to increase the room in the bust, you wouldn't want to place the ruler so that it removed ⅛" (3 mm) or more from the bust area. Keeping the fullness at the bust might require slightly reshaping the blend under the bust in order to get a smooth transition. In these instances, choose the scenario that makes the most sense for the body you are fitting.

Working with a Straight Edge Ruler

With experimentation, you'll find a straight edge ruler that you like to work with. The thickness and the flexibility of the ruler will influence how comfortable it is in your hand. The fashion ruler has a straight edge on one side, but the ruler is rigid and thick. I like to use 2" × 18" (5.1 × 45.7 cm) and 1" × 6" (2.5 × 15.2 cm) flexible rulers marked in ⅛" (3 mm) increments. The markings form a grid, which is useful to check lines that need to be perpendicular to each other.

Use a straight edge ruler to draw lines such as the horizontal balance line, the grainline, and center front, as well as any other seam line that needs to be straight. I also use these flexible rulers with grids to accurately measure and mark seam allowances.

Working with the Fashion Ruler

1 The fashion ruler is quite versatile and produces a wide variety of shaped lines, especially because it can be used in four different orientations. Sometimes the solution to blending a seam is to flip the ruler over.

2 To find the best area of the ruler to use when blending seam lines, slide the ruler back and forth a few inches (cm), rather than picking up the ruler. Seeing a potential blend that is not very good along with a choice of blends often helps you to find the area of the ruler that is effective.

3 If you want less fullness, use a flatter part of the ruler.

4 If you want to add more fullness, use a rounder part of the ruler. Note that with this ruler position you'll need to blend a second time lower down in order to smoothly transition to the seam line below in the area indicated by the arrow.

FINESSE THE CURVE

While learning to use the fashion ruler to draw seam lines, it is sometimes difficult to visualize the shape of the seam while also trying to find the corresponding part of the ruler that will produce the shape. When this happens, lightly draw the line freehand, and then use the ruler to finalize and finesse the line.

blending seam lines

To get long and gentle blends, position the fashion ruler so that as much of it as possible touches the lines to be blended. In achieving a long blend, you often will need to reshape a part of the seam slightly. Experiment with ruler positions to do this.

1 Since many patterns do not include seam lines, draw in all original seam lines.

2 This ruler position smoothly blends the tick marks of the new seam near the waist, but the transition to the lower straight portion of the new seam (marked in red) is not good.

3 In comparison, this ruler position nicely blends the straight lower portion of the side seam with the first few tick marks of the new seam line. Once the initial transition has been made, the rest of the seam can be blended, as follows.

4 This ruler position is okay, but does not pick up the fullness in the hip curve.

5 In comparison, this ruler position shows the fullness of the hip and nicely blends into the rest of the new seam line.

6 The new blended seam (in red).

adding seam allowances

After fine-tuning a seam line, add the seam allowance. The amount of seam allowance is your choice as the patternmaker. If you use varying seam allowances for different types of garments or within one garment, clearly mark your pattern.

1 For a straight seam, measure the desired seam allowance using a ruler for accuracy and draw the cut line (in blue).

2 On curved lines, it's often best to mark the seam allowance with a series of tick marks.

3 Then blend the curved cut line with a fashion ruler.

4 Once the cut line is drawn in, trim away the excess paper.

lengthening and shortening patterns and grainline arrows

LENGTHENING AND SHORTENING

It is best to lengthen and shorten patterns at or near the location where you made the alteration on the fitting muslin. This is typically done above or below the HBL in order to preserve the reference point that the HBL provides.

There are two types of length adjustments: even adjustments alter the pattern the same amount across the pattern piece; uneven adjustments alter the pattern a different amount on one side of the pattern piece compared to the other side. Both adjustments are made across the entire pattern piece in accordance with good patternmaking practices; this keeps the pattern flat.

Even Adjustments: Tucks and Spreads

Make even adjustments using a tuck to shorten the pattern and a spread to lengthen the pattern. It's easiest to make even adjustments parallel to the horizontal balance line.

1 Mark the placement of the adjustment on the pattern. Position the pattern so that the grainline is along a grid and so that the placement mark is at a cross grid. Use this cross grid to draw the adjustment line.

2 For a tuck, which shortens the pattern, measure and mark the amount of the adjustment, and draw a line here that is parallel to the adjustment line. The part of the pattern between these lines indicates the amount to be removed.

(continued)

ACCURATE TUCKS

To keep your pattern flat and precise, cut and tape the pattern when making a tuck adjustment rather than making a fold in the pattern paper.

3 Extend the grainline so it is marked on both sides of the adjustment.

4 Cut the pattern apart along either line. Lay one cut line on top of the other, matching them precisely and keeping the grainline of each pattern segment aligned on the same grid line. Tape the pattern pieces together.

5 If necessary, blend the seam lines and the cut lines. In this example, both the center back seam and the back princess seam need slight blending.

6 The finished pattern.

7 For a spread, which lengthens the pattern, cut the pattern apart along the adjustment line. Add paper to one side of the separated pattern; it doesn't matter which side.

8 Measure and mark the amount of the adjustment, drawing a line parallel to the adjustment line.

9 Extend the grainline on the added paper. Here I use the center front line as the grainline because the grainline arrow marked on the pattern is too close to the edge of the pattern and the seam line to be easily recognizable.

10 Align the other segment of the pattern with the new adjustment line that indicates the amount of the spread, matching the grainline arrow, and tape in place.

11 The blended and finished pattern.

Uneven Adjustments: Open-Wedges and Close-Wedges

Make uneven adjustments using a wedge, which can either lengthen or shorten a pattern. Only make wedge adjustments on pattern pieces that have seams on both sides. It is not possible to make a wedge adjustment when one side of the pattern is the center front or is on the fold. This is because a wedge adjustment causes both sides of the pattern to bend, and these two situations require a straight line.

To make wedge adjustments, transfer the placement of the wedge from the muslin to the pattern. Wedge adjustments do not need to be parallel to the HBL or perpendicular to the grainline.

1 When making either an open-wedge or close-wedge, start by marking the placement of the wedge adjustment at each side of the pattern along the seam lines. Draw a line between the marks using a straight edge ruler. Note that it's important to mark wedge adjustments on the seam line, not on the cut line of the pattern.

2 To lengthen the pattern with an open-wedge adjustment, cut along the adjustment line, starting at the side of the pattern that will be lengthened or shortened. Cut to, but not through, the opposite seam line.

3 On the side of the pattern where the wedge adjustment ends, cut through the seam allowance up to the seam line, leaving a hinge of paper at the seam line.

Here you can see the fold line "breaking" in the attempt to make an impossible wedge.

4 Spread the cut portion of the pattern and tape in additional paper on one portion of the pattern. On the added paper, measure and mark the amount of the spread, which in this example is ⅝" (1.6 cm).

5 Bring the free side of the pattern to the mark on the added paper made in the previous step, and secure the pattern with tape. The pattern paper should be absolutely flat.

6 Blend the vertical seams on each side of the pattern and, lastly, adjust the seam allowances.
(continued)

7 To shorten the pattern with a close-wedge adjustment, measure and mark the amount of the closure along the seam line where the pattern has been cut. Draw a line from the mark indicating the amount of the closure to the hinge mark on the opposite side of the pattern.

8 Cut a hinge, as described above, along one of the adjustment lines. Move one side of the pattern to make it overlap the other pattern piece by rotating the paper at the hinge point, bringing the wedge lines together. It doesn't matter which portion of the pattern is moved on top of the other. The pattern paper should be absolutely flat. Tape the pattern in place.

9 Blend the vertical seams on each side of the pattern and then adjust the seam allowances.

UNUSUAL CURVED CENTER FRONT SEAMS

Occasionally an unusual garment design has a curved center front seam. This is the only exception where a wedge adjustment can involve the center front seam.

GRAINLINE ARROWS

After making open-wedge and close-wedge adjustments, redraw the grainline arrow. This is almost always done by extending the grainline from the lower portion of the pattern through the upper portion of the pattern. The logic of this is evident if you think back to a plaid skirt. Since the hem of the garment must remain parallel to the floor and perpendicular to the grainline, it's the upper portion of the garment above the HBL that is allowed to go off grain.

On bodices, allowing the upper portion of the garment to be a bit off-grain often improves how the garment fits. This is because fabric on a slight bias grain tends to mold to the body more readily than fabric on the straight of grain.

However, when making adjustments to sleeves, the grainline arrow is extended downward from the sleeve cap. This preserves the grainline in the upper portion of the sleeve. On a long sleeve, the lower portion will be a bit off-grain, which often helps the sleeve follow the natural curvature of the arm.

ADJUSTMENTS TO ADJOINING PATTERN PIECES

If you perform any length adjustments to one pattern piece, the adjoining pattern piece must also be adjusted to keep the seam lines the same length. It is important to keep this rule in mind during the fitting process. A common length adjustment is a tuck and wedge combination, as shown in the examples below. In the photographs of fitting garments, you will see that this occurs in many different areas of the garment and in different combinations of manipulations, such as tucks, wedges, and increased dart intakes.

One way to shorten the center back of a princess seam garment in relation to the front is to make an even tuck in the center back pattern, and then make a wedge on the side back panel that goes to nothing at the side seam, where the length adjustment ends.

Before making a tuck and close-wedge combination.

After making a tuck and close-wedge combination.

Before making a spread and open-wedge combination.

After making a spread and open-wedge combination.

walking and truing a pattern

Seams that will be sewn together need to be the same length, unless there is a specific reason to vary their lengths, in which case the fabric is either eased or stretched in the sewing process. It's relatively simple to compare two straight seams, but if one or both seams are curved, it's more difficult. To compare two seam lines with complete accuracy, they should be "walked." The process of comparing seam lengths and making adjustments so that the adjoining seams are exactly the same length is called "truing."

When walking two adjoining pattern pieces, the seam lines are compared. It's important to focus on the seam line and ignore any seam allowance or cut lines. If you are working with a pattern that intentionally does not have seam allowances, as in most couture sewing, be sure to note that the seam line is most likely the edge of the paper.

WHERE TO BEGIN THE PROCESS

If the pattern pieces have an HBL that intersects the seams being checked, start the process at the HBL, since it is a fixed point. Side seams of a bodice are a good example. Walk the seams from the HBL to the underarm, and then repeat the process from the HBL to the hem.

For other pattern pieces that do not have an intersecting HBL, start at a notch if there is one. A shoulder seam is a good example: start at the notch and walk the seams to the neck, and then repeat the process from the notch to the shoulder.

If there is no fixed point at which to start, you will need to make an educated decision about where to begin. I often start at the hem of the garment and walk the seam up, or I start at the outer edge of the garment and walk the seam toward the inner edge of the garment.

1 Lay one pattern on top of the other, matching the seam lines. Anchor the patterns with a pin through the seam line at the starting point, which in this case is the HBL. You can see that the bottom of this pattern already walks correctly since the top and bottom pattern pieces match from the HBL down to the hem of the garment.

2 Where the two seam lines diverge, place another pin directly on the seam. Note that the two cut edges also diverge.

3 Remove the first pin, and pivot the top pattern so that the seams are brought into alignment starting at the pin. Where the two seams diverge, place another pin; repeat the process to the end of the seam.

4 In this example, the notches line up nicely on the two pattern pieces. After walking the entire seam, note any discrepancy in the seam lengths: here the bottom pattern is approximately $\frac{1}{8}$" (3 mm) longer than the top pattern.

ADJUSTING SEAMS WITH DISCREPANCIES

If the two seam lines are not the same length and they should be (that is, there is no ease built into the pattern), then you have to make an educated decision about which seam to adjust. Knowing the intent of what was being done in the fitting is a good guide. For instance, if I'm widening a neckline on a garment and the shoulder seams are not true, then I would cut off the excess of the longer piece at the neck. If I were making the neckline fit closer to the neck, then I would add to the shorter piece at the neck. If the discrepancy is ½" (1.3 cm) or more, then splitting the difference is always safe. Cut off ¼" (6 mm) from the long piece, and add ¼" (6 mm) to the short piece.

Since I frequently will sew another test garment after such pattern alterations, I'll have the opportunity to check that what I have done in the pattern work makes sense on the body.

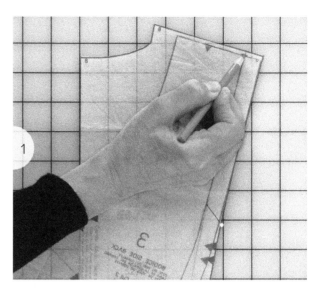

1 Continuing the example, I will cut off the excess length from the bottom pattern, which is ⅛" (3 mm) longer when walked. First, mark the bottom pattern. Normally this would be done at the seam line, but in this case, there is such a small and obvious adjustment, it is okay to make the adjustment at the cut line.

2 Blend the new cut line, going to nothing along the shoulder toward the neck. In this example, it is only the princess seam that needs to be changed.

3 Cut away the excess paper.

WALKING PATTERNS WITH DARTS

When truing a pattern with darts, skip the area between the dart legs, since the dart will be sewn before the two pattern pieces are joined. If you prefer, fold the dart out in the paper before walking the pattern; note that this can make walking the seams a bit awkward, as the pattern piece will not lie flat on the table.

1 Have the pattern piece without the dart on top of the pattern piece with the dart. Walk the pattern pieces up to the lower dart leg. Mark the lower dart leg placement along the seam line.

2 Shift the top pattern piece so that the mark indicating the lower dart leg matches the upper dart leg at the seam line. Then finish walking the seam.

KEEPING PATTERNS ACCURATE

I like to execute pattern work as accurately as possible and rarely have more than $\frac{1}{16}$" to $\frac{1}{8}$" (1.6 to 3.0 mm) of discrepancy. You will need to decide what degree of accuracy is important to you. Many sewers say that working from a trued pattern makes sewing a garment quite a bit faster.

placing and creating notches

Notches are tools to help you sew the garment pieces together accurately. Sewing is like a puzzle. You have a number of pieces that go together, and notches help you put the puzzle together correctly. In the same way, notches are useful tools when doing pattern work.

There are some traditional notch usages. For instance, one notch on a sleeve indicates the sleeve front, and two notches indicate the sleeve back. These will correspond to the one notch on the garment front armhole and the two notches on the garment back armhole. With some commercial patterns, there is a recognizable system of how notches are used. As you take control of your pattern work, you might find you need fewer notches on some garments and many more on other garments. Remember that notches are tools—utilize them according to your needs.

ADDING A NOTCH TO A PATTERN

Notches are used in two primary ways. First, they are used to indicate which pattern or garment sections are adjoining. Notches are extremely helpful when two or more pattern pieces look similar and when there are lots of pattern pieces for a garment. For example, on a skirt pattern with princess lines, the placement and number of notches used in one location make it impossible to mistakenly sew garment sections together that are not adjoining. Second, notches are used to control where ease is put in a garment, which I discuss in detail in the following section.

1 To add a notch to a pattern, draw the placement of the new notch on one of the two adjoining pattern pieces. Place the other pattern piece on top, matching up two pre-existing notches.

2 Accurately walk the top pattern piece, stopping when you come to the new notch and drawing it in on the upper pattern piece.

adjusting patterns with built-in ease

Occasionally a garment fits better when two adjoining seams are not exactly the same length, but rather one seam is slightly longer than the other. The excess in the longer seam is referred to as "ease," since it is eased into the shorter seam during the sewing process. For example, on a princess line bodice, the side front princess seam often has a small amount of ease in relation to the front princess seam. This bit of ease helps fit a rounded bust shape. When there is built-in ease such as this, notches indicate to the sewer the specific portion of the seam where the ease should occur.

REPOSITIONING BUILT-IN EASE

To adjust the placement of built-in ease in a pattern, use notches to control where the ease is distributed on the adjoining pattern piece. In the following example, the front princess seam is true from the HBL up to the lower notches, and from the armhole down to the upper notches. When the patterns are walked between the notches, the side front is ⅜" (1 cm) longer than the front, which means there is ⅜" (1 cm) of ease.

If distributing the ease across a greater distance enhances the fit, move the corresponding notches on the adjoining pattern pieces. For instance, the lower notches of this pattern could be moved downward ½" (1.3 cm). This allows the total amount of ease to remain the same, but it is distributed over a greater distance.

REMOVING BUILT-IN EASE

Sometimes patterns have more built-in ease than is desirable. On a princess bodice, for example, smaller and more pointed bust shapes require less ease than fuller and rounder busts. And if a princess line garment fits very well, there is often no need for any ease at all. Also, some fabrics, such as taffeta weaves and polished cottons, are extremely difficult to ease. In these cases, take control of your pattern and reduce or eliminate the amount of ease to get a nice looking finished garment.

1 With the pattern containing the ease on top, walk along the seam line from the notches to the end of the seam containing the ease, which in this case is at the armhole. At the end of the seam, mark the position of the seam line from the bottom pattern onto the top pattern (in red).

2 On the top pattern, blend the new seam line to the existing seam line.

3 Correct the seam allowance and trim along the new cut line.

4 Then, reposition the notch that indicated the location of the ease. In this case, reposition the notch that is closest to the armhole on the side front pattern. To do this, walk the side front pattern to the front pattern starting at the armhole. When you come to the notch on the front pattern, mark the side front pattern.

truing difficult seams

When walking two adjoining pattern pieces, you occasionally will encounter situations as you approach the end of the seam where it is unclear what the pattern pieces should look like. This is most common when the seam on each adjoining pattern piece is shaped differently, as is the case with an armscye princess seam or when the intersecting seam is steeply angled. In these types of situations, many commercial patterns square off one of the seam allowances or provide a match point at the termination of the seam itself. However, truing your pattern precisely makes sewing the garment much easier.

Anytime that I cannot visualize what the ends of two adjoining seams should look like, I "stack" my pattern pieces so that they mimic how the seams would look as if they were sewn.

STACKING PATTERNS

1 After walking this back princess seam from the notches (in red) up to the armhole, it is difficult to see what will line up with what when sewing the seams together.

2 To clarify this, pin the pattern pieces together as though sewing the seam. Note that sometimes you can only pin the top inch (cm) or so if the seam is very curved.

3 Fold back the top pattern piece to see what the seam intersection would look like if it were sewn. In this example, you can see that the side back pattern is the wrong shape and doesn't extend enough, leaving a small gap, as indicated by the arrow.

4 To correct this, tape on additional paper to the side back pattern.

5 Fold back the side back pattern again. If it's helpful, pin it in place to prevent the patterns from shifting. Blend the seam, drawing across the patterns where they join.

6 Add the seam allowance (in blue).

(continued)

7 Cut along the new cut line. This is the trued armhole.

8 Unpin and trim off excess paper along the princess seam.

9 The tops of the adjoining princess patterns might look odd because commercial patterns do not usually true their seams like this. However, placing a ruler on top of the pattern clarifies the seam line.

10 The seam will now match perfectly when sewing the princess seams.

moving a seam

When a seam requires repositioning during a fitting, this can be reflected on the fitting muslin in two ways: you can release the seam and re-pin it in the new location, or you can indicate the new placement of the seam by drawing a line. Establishing a notch placement in both cases makes the pattern work more accurate, as you will see below.

REPOSITIONING BY PINNING IN THE FITTING

1 Before unpinning the muslin, mark the pin placement (black) and create a new notch on the muslin (green). To create the notch, simply draw a short line perpendicular to the seam. It should clearly show on each of the adjoining garment sections. Then unpin and press the muslin flat.

2 Transfer the new seam placement (red) and the notch (red) to the pattern. Adjust the seam allowances along the shoulder seam and cut along the new cut line.

3 Stack the patterns to true the neckline intersection as follows: Fold one of the pattern pieces along the shoulder seam line; it doesn't matter which one. Align this seam with the adjoining shoulder seam, matching the new notch. Pin the pattern pieces together. In this example, the neckline seams match but the cut lines do not.

4 To true the cut lines, add seam allowance on the front pattern piece at the shoulder, as follows: Draw the intersecting neckline and armhole seam lines, and add the seam allowances. This is what the pattern pieces look like when finished.

REPOSITIONING BY DRAWING IN THE FITTING

Note that in this example the center front is on the fold.

1 On this fitting muslin, the blue line was drawn on the muslin during the fitting, indicating the new position of the shoulder seam. Measure the distance between the existing seam and the new seam placement. In this example, the shoulder seam is being moved forward ⅝" (1.6 cm) at the armhole and ¾" (1.9 cm) at the neckline. Draw a notch (green) on the muslin through the new and existing seam lines somewhere along the shoulder seam.

2 Before moving the seam position on the pattern, pick up the new notch from the previous step at the original seams on each pattern piece.

3 To reposition the front seam, measure and mark the position of the new seam line on the patterns. Draw the new front seam using a straight edge ruler.

4 Add the seam allowance to the front shoulder seam. Extend the notch, if necessary, so it intersects with the cut line. Cut along the cut line.

5 The back seam line is being moved forward, so you will need to tape in extra paper on the pattern. Measure, mark, and draw the position of the new seam line (in red) as was done for the front. Add the seam allowance for the back shoulder seam. Extend the notch, if necessary. Cut along the cut line of the shoulder seam.

6 Proceed with truing the intersecting seam lines by stacking the patterns as follows: Fold one pattern piece along the shoulder seam line. Match the notch marked in the first step. Note that the original notches along the shoulder seam are no longer valid due to the change in shoulder seam placement, which is why it's so important to establish the new notch. Reblend the seams and cut lines, if necessary, and cut along new cut lines.

PATTERNMAKING TIP

If there is a fitting adjustment on a seam that also needs to be repositioned, do the pattern work in separate steps. For instance, if a shoulder seam needs to be taken in as well as repositioned, first make the pattern changes to take the seam in. Then make the pattern changes to reposition the seam. Working methodically is the best way to prevent confusion.

moving a dart

The theory of dart manipulation in flat pattern development allows you to move a dart from its original location to a new location. Moving a dart position can be useful in order to get a better or more attractive fit. The ability to move the dart location on the pattern is also helpful when fitting, because then it's possible to pin out excess fabric where the excess occurs, which facilitates getting the optimum fit. Then, if you don't want a dart in that location on the body, it can be moved to a more flattering position.

When a dart is relocated, the fit is not substantively changed in the relocation process, although it's best to check and fine-tune the fit in a test garment.

In the fitting examples, I often move a dart to a location I prefer by manipulating the fabric, which is called "draping." Draping a dart during a fitting and transferring the dart in pattern work both produce good results. Some people prefer one method over the other, but many people use both methods depending on what is expedient in a given situation.

Some dart transfers are done at the apex, meaning that the apex becomes the rotation point where a hinge is created and around which the dart is moved. The dart point can also be used as the rotation point in simple situations, such as the example to the right.

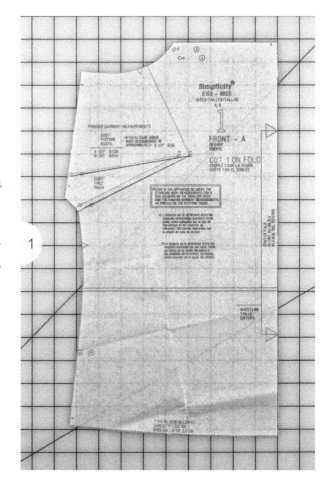

1 Draw the new dart position (in red). Here the dart is being moved from the bust to the armhole on a tank top.

2 Cut through the original dart (it's okay to cut along either one of the dart legs or through the middle of the dart) up to, but not through, the transfer point. Also cut along the line for the new dart up to, but not through, the transfer point; this creates a hinge. Rotate the dart intake to the new position by bringing the two original dart legs together, and tape in place.

3 Trim off the old dart extension. Tape in additional paper at the new dart legs, making sure that it extends well beyond the dart. The dart legs must be trued in order to create a new dart extension, which is discussed in the following section.

truing dart legs

Truing a dart ensures that both dart legs are the same length. The process of truing a dart will form a perfect dart extension, which is the area of the pattern between the dart legs at the intersecting seam. Working with trued darts makes the task of sewing darts easier and promotes accuracy.

When truing a dart in the pattern, fold the dart in the direction that it will be pressed in the fabric. Vertical darts, such as waist darts and neck darts, are traditionally pressed toward the center front or center back of the garment. Horizontal darts, such as side bust darts and elbow darts, are traditionally pressed down toward the hem of the garment.

Determine the direction the dart will be pressed. If the dart will be pressed down, begin the process of truing the dart legs with the lower dart leg. If the dart will be pressed toward the center of the garment, begin the process of truing the dart legs with the dart leg that is closest to the center.

SHAPED DARTS

Shaped darts, which have curved dart legs, often improve the fit of a garment. However, it's very difficult to match curved dart legs when truing a pattern. Therefore, with all darts that intersect a seam, draft the dart legs with a straight edge ruler to facilitate truing the dart legs. Then draw the curved dart legs or make a note on the pattern to sew curved darts.

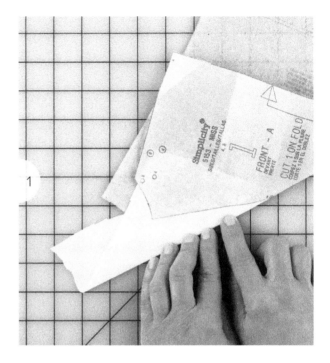

1 Fold the pattern paper along the selected dart leg.

2 Bring the folded dart leg to the other dart leg, pivoting the paper at the dart point. It's helpful to work on the corner of a table, having the dart on the table surface and letting the rest of the pattern hang off the table. Pin or temporarily tape the dart closed.

3 Reposition the pattern so that the dart area is flat on the table, and reblend the intersecting seam and cut line, if necessary. Here it is only necessary to correct the cut line.

4 Cut the pattern along the cut line. Unpin the dart. When the dart is opened up, the dart legs will be perfectly trued.

scaling patterns up and down

In many of the fitting examples, I fit the garments fairly close to the body, which is what I think of as a clean but not a tight fit. This allows me to actually address all of the fitting issues, since with a stylistically loose garment, it can be difficult to distinguish between a fitting issue and the largeness of the garment.

If the client intends to wear a layer under the garment that is being fit, have her wear this layering garment during all of the fitting sessions. See page 39 for more information.

Once you have a pattern that fits well, it's easy to scale the pattern up and down. For instance, you can scale a blouse up to a jacket or scale a jacket down to a blouse. The theory of how to do this is shown in the illustration below.

For princess seam garments, first start with these changes made to the perimeter of the garment. To make the garment roomier still, add a small amount (perhaps ⅛" [3 mm]) to the princess seams themselves.

Make the following adjustments to scale a blouse pattern up to a jacket or a jacket pattern up to a coat. To scale a blouse pattern to a coat, double the measurements. The measurements can also be used to scale a pattern down by making these adjustments in reverse.

working in an efficient order

Deciding what order to use when making pattern changes might seem overwhelming at first. To simplify the process, try to limit the number of changes you make on each test garment. Making three or four pattern changes at one time is much easier than making ten or twelve.

Limiting the number of changes does mean that you will make more test garments, which may seem like a lot of work. However, fitting multiple clean muslins allows you to check that the changes you've just made are working. And fitting a clean muslin also makes it easier to see the remaining fitting issues.

It is most efficient to first make pattern adjustments that affect the interior of the pattern, and then make changes to the perimeter of the pattern. If you make pattern changes in a different order, no harm is done. The end result will be the same, but you'll find yourself blending and truing some seams more than once, and you'll probably have more bits and pieces of paper taped to the pattern.

As you gain experience and confidence in altering patterns, you'll develop your own work habits that put you in control of the pattern. It's more important to work cleanly and methodically than it is to follow a specific order.

GENERAL ORDER FOR PATTERN WORK

1 Make length adjustments, such as horizontal tucks and wedges.

2 Make width adjustments, including reshaping vertical seams, adjusting the bust area, and reworking waist darts.

3 Fine-tune the placement of the shoulder seam and side seam.

4 True dart legs.

5 Fine-tune the placement and shape of the neck, armhole, and waist seam.

6 Blend seam lines if not done above.

7 Walk and true seams.

8 Measure seam allowances and draw cut lines.

9 Cut along cut lines.

FITTING PROJECTS

This chapter shows the process of fitting three different garments from start to finish, which is important in order to understand the flow of a fitting. It is organized by the type of garment being fit. The style lines in these garments are those most commonly used, such as a bodice with side bust darts and a bodice with princess lines.

SKIRT

A straight skirt is the easiest garment to fit, because it's the simplest garment to understand conceptually. Visualizing a plaid skirt helps establish the fitting axis in your mind, which is useful when fitting other garments as well.

STYLE/FITTING CONSIDERATIONS

It's best to fit a straight skirt with the skirt anchored at the natural or true waist (the smallest part of the torso). If you prefer to wear your skirt lower, as many women do, this is a stylistic change and is done after the skirt has been fit at the waist. Fitting at the natural waist allows the skirt to settle on the body, resulting in an excellent fit. If the skirt is lower on the torso, it often shifts on the body during the fitting process.

Front darts are typically used to narrow the skirt circumference from the hip to the waist, as well as to fit the body. As shown in the process below, front darts are not always flattering and can be eliminated.

Whether to use a waistband or a waist facing is a stylistic consideration; the fit of the skirt is the same. The comfort of the wearer is another factor, in conjunction with what works the best for her body type.

PROCESS OF FITTING THE SKIRT

1 Tie a piece of elastic around the body at the waist of the skirt. The elastic will naturally find the smallest part of the torso. The elastic does not need to be exactly at the waist seam of the muslin. Assess the circumference of the garment at the hip.

2 If there is too much ease, pin out the excess, leaving enough wearing ease. If there is not enough ease, release the seam; remember, it is not good fitting practice to fit a muslin that is too tight. Begin the process of getting the HBL level. Place a yardstick (meterstick) against the buttocks and note where the HBL falls. Marking the yardstick (meterstick) with a piece of tape provides an easy-to-see reference point.

3 Check the HBL at the side of the skirt.

4 If the HBL is low, gently pull at the waist of the skirt, bringing the HBL to its proper level. If the HBL is high, gently pull at the hem of the skirt.

5 Check the front of the skirt, bringing the HBL level. Continue this process until you are certain that the HBL is level all the way around the skirt. You are establishing your fitting axis, so accuracy is important.

(continued)

FITTING TIP

If the HBL continues to move as you measure and remeasure, the skirt may be too tight (usually across the buttock or high hip), or the skirt fabric may be "crawling" against the fabric of the bodice. Releasing tight areas and having some slack or blousing in the bodice solves these problems.

6 Assess the total dart intake on one half of the skirt back. Pinching out the dart amount on both sides at the same time will prevent pulling the center back seam to one side. Determine how many darts to use. Because the total dart intake here is large, use two smaller darts.

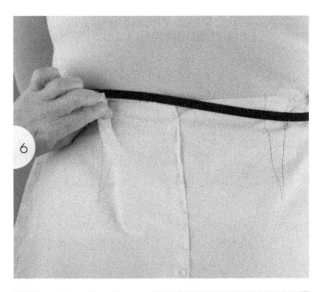

7 The dart placement should be visually attractive and provide a good fit. Finding the roundest part of the buttocks and marking the dart points facilitates draping in the darts. The two pins mark the dart points just above the fleshiest part of the buttocks.

8 Drape in the darts, following the contours of the body. This takes practice. Let your fingers "read" the body. Pinching the fabric at the top and bottom of the dart can be helpful. Note that this dart placement does not follow the dart specified by the pattern. However, having the pattern's dart placement drawn on the muslin provides a good point of reference when draping in the other side.

FITTING TIP

Darts with large intakes look ungainly on the body. If a single dart intake is greater than 1¼" (3.2 cm), you get better results splitting the dart intake between two darts.

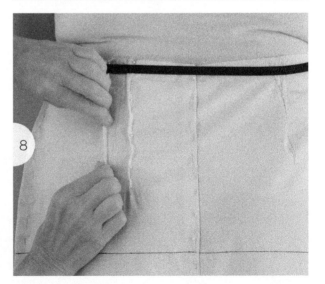

9 After draping and pinning the darts, check the HBL and bring it back to position.

10 Commercial skirt patterns typically use front darts to reduce the circumference of the skirt at the waist relative to the hip. Front darts are flattering on some figures, but not on others. Experimenting with darts and their placement is the best way to get a flattering fit. When the darts are pinned using this pattern's placement, the roundness of this client's stomach is visually accentuated.

11 If the darts are moved toward the side seam, the waist looks quite wide in proportion to the hip.

(continued)

THE FUNCTION OF A DART

The function of a dart is to create three-dimensional space in the garment. The dart should point toward the fullest part of the fleshy mound that this space will accommodate. Place the dart points just before the fleshiest part of the mound. If dart points extend beyond the mound (where the body begins to taper off), the dart creates space that will not be filled by the body; the result is unattractive.

12 The client and the fitter agreed that having no darts in the front was the most flattering. The equivalent of the front dart intake can be removed from the pattern at the side seam Recheck the HBL.

13 Check that the side seam hangs straight. The side seam should be positioned approximately at the person's side and placed to make the body look proportionate. In this example, if the side seam were moved forward, it would make the stomach look smaller, but then it would fall to the front of the leg. One is not "right" and the other "wrong"; it's a judgment call the fitter makes.

14 Move the elastic so that it follows the client's natural curvature at the waist and creates a smooth line. Draw under the elastic to mark the client's waist.

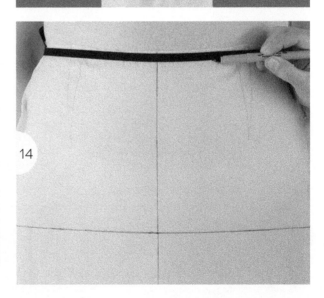

PLACEMENT OF THE SIDE SEAM

Get help determining where the side seam should be. Ask the person you're fitting to close her eyes and put her thumbs on her sides at waist level. This tells you what she considers to be the middle of her body, and it's almost always accurate. You can make a visual assessment from there.

15 Have the client sit to check tightness and comfort. If the skirt is too tight, there will be pull lines in the cloth radiating from the side seam toward the middle of the skirt. As in this example, no wrinkles means there's adequate ease.

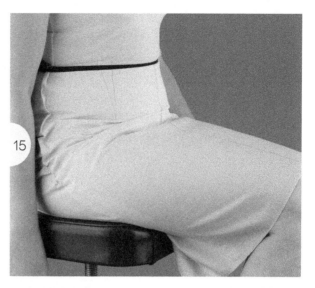

16 If the skirt fits well and doesn't require a second muslin, establish the actual waist of the skirt. This is a combination of what the client wants and what is visually pleasing. Some women prefer a lower waistline, often near the navel. Use a piece of cording or ribbon to help you establish the new waist placement. If the waistline is too straight, it makes the skirt look unflattering and like it's falling off the hips.

17 A slightly curved waistline is usually more flattering and natural looking.

PATTERN WORK EXAMPLES

See Altering Patterns (page 61) for basic pattern-making techniques.

Waist Adjustments

The front waist seam drawn, with the front dart eliminated (**A**).

The back waist with the dart legs trued (**B**).

Hip Curve Differences

For many figures, the front and back hip curves are slightly different, because the back waist is often smaller than the front waist (**C**).

BODICE WITH DARTS

Side bust darts are an excellent fitting tool. Like all darts, they add dimensionality to a garment. To understand this concept of dimensionality, take a sheet of paper and fold a dart in it so that the dart point is somewhere in the middle of the page. Then put the paper on a table. The paper no longer lies flat but looks like a pup-tent, arcing above the table with space underneath. In a bodice, the three-dimensional space created by the dart provides room for the bust to sit within. And this is what allows the front of the garment to hang straight rather than flaring away from the body at the hem.

STYLE/FITTING CONSIDERATIONS

Bustlines vary in shape as well as in size. Some women's breasts are pointed, others are rounded. Some women have a lot of breast tissue on the side of the bust; others have a deep bust, top to bottom. Some women are "hollow" above the bust; others have a prominent chest structure. All of these variations must be taken into account during the fitting process.

Some figures are harder to fit nicely than others with a darted pattern. Using two parallel darts might help, especially on fuller bustlines. If you're having a lot of trouble, consider switching to a pattern that has princess lines. A shoulder princess line is an excellent fitting tool and works very well for all figure types and bust shapes.

Bust darts can be "straight" and level, or they can emanate from the side seam at any angle you wish. Their position impacts the way the garment looks on the body. In all cases, the dart should point toward the apex or the fullest part of the bust.

Without a dart, the fabric flares away from the body at the hemline.

With a dart, the fabric no longer flares away from the body.

The length of the dart will vary according to the bust shape and size. As a rule of thumb, the smaller the bust, the closer the dart point will be to the apex. The larger the bust, the farther away the dart point will be to the apex.

PROCESS OF FITTING THE BODICE WITH SIDE BUST DART

1 The bodice front. Note the drag lines emanating from the bust. They are especially noticeable above the bust ending in the gaping armhole and below the bust ending at the side seam just below the HBL.

2 The bodice back. Note that the back of the arm is crushing or pushing down on the fabric at the back armhole. This indicates that the back of the garment is too wide and that the back armhole needs to be clipped. Another way to conceptualize this is that the back armhole seam is not in the correct place, but needs to be farther in on the garment. This is equivalent to a tightness issue and must be addressed at the very beginning of the fitting process.

3 The bodice back after the armhole is clipped, which allows the fabric across the mid-back to relax. Note that there are still folds of fabric at the underarm, which suggest that there might be excess girth at the underarm. There is also excess fabric above the HBL. Address the fit at the bust and get the HBL level before moving on to the girth issue. At this time, you could temporarily pin the back to bring the HBL to level.

4 Increase the side bust dart intake by removing the stitching of the existing dart and draping a new dart, and pin an armscye dart to eliminate the drag lines identified in step 1. The armscye dart is usually rotated into the side bust dart in the pattern work. Note that the model's body has tilted due to the position of her arm.

5 Pin a tuck above the HBL across the entire back, making the HBL level. The tuck intake equaled the amount that the side bust dart was increased, which is very often the case.

6 Now check the amount of fabric at the underarm identified in step 3. Although I am pinching ⅝" to ¾" (1.6 to 1.9 cm) from each seam allowance, how much I pin out will depend on how fitted the client wants the garment to be.

7 When pinning out the excess girth, do so in a way that keeps the side seam straight. In this case, the back seam line remained the same, and all of the excess was taken out on the front. It's important to "let the fabric tell you what to do." I released the side seam at the underarm and then experimented to see where the excess girth actually was, using the position and straightness of the side seam as a guide.

8 If the side seam is taken in, as was done in step 7, check the back and front armholes again for tightness, clipping more deeply if necessary. This back armhole required more clipping; slowly we are discovering where the back armhole seam really needs to be. See pattern work on page 118.

9 Pin out the excess in the side seam from the HBL to the hem. Also note the slight looseness just below the underarm on the back. Even though the front side seam was taken in at bust level to reduce the total girth, this looseness shows that the garment is still not tight. This is partly because more space was provided for the bust when the side bust dart intake was increased. Take in the side seam more if you want a tight fit.

(continued)

10 The muslin is starting to fit much better. For beginners, this would be a good time to transfer the fitting changes to the pattern and make a new test garment. Continuing with the fitting process, now that there are not so many distracting fitting issues, note that the HBL on the left back is slightly lower than on the right. Also note that the left armhole is slightly crumpled. Both are indications that the left shoulder is lower than the right.

11 To make the shoulders even for the fitting process, pin out the excess along the left shoulder seam; follow the contour of the shoulder line, making the HBL level while taking care not to overfit. Alternatively, use a shoulder pad on the low side only. Moving to other fitting issues, note that there is excess fabric at the small of the back.

12 Assess how much excess fabric there is in the small of the back—quite a lot.

13 One option for eliminating the excess fabric is to pin it out along the center back seam, as shown here. Below the HBL, the diagonal drag lines that point to the center back seam are due to the large amount that was taken out right at the small of the back.

14 Another option is to take a small amount out along the center back seam and add waist darts. Taper the waist darts to nothing a few inches (cm) below prominent shoulder blades for a flattering fit. The amount you pin out depends on how closely fitted you want the garment to be. See pattern work on page 118.

15 Note that the back neck stands slightly away from the model's body. This indicates the need for neck darts, which frequently make the garment more comfortable and prevent the garment from shifting around on the body.

16 Drape in and pin the neck darts, following the contours of the body. Note that the right and left upper backs are different, which is accentuated by the way each dart has been draped. To help the model look balanced and even, I would make both darts the same, using the left back neck dart in the pattern work. Also note the slight drag lines between the center back seam and the prominent right shoulder blade.

17 Let out the center back seam, starting about 2" (5.1 cm) below the neck and tapering to nothing a few inches (cm) above the HBL. This allows the fabric to relax and reduces the drag lines noted in step 16.

(continued)

18 To establish the armhole placement, find the back and front "crease." This is where the arm attaches to the body. I have folded back the test garment fabric to reveal the back crease.

19 Mark the back crease.

20 Mark the front crease.

21 Establish the placement of the armhole at the shoulder so that it makes the body look proportionate. This is a judgment call. The most flattering placement is often farther up along the shoulder line than the "hinge" of the shoulder, which is the traditional landmark. These shoulder seams, indicated by the black tape, are too far out in my opinion, and the placement makes the model's shoulders look disproportionately broad.

22 To my eye, this armhole placement is too far in, making the model's hips and waist look large.

23 This placement, in my opinion, is the most flattering. Draw the armhole placement from the shoulder seam to the front and back crease.

24 Establish the underarm. A high under-arm provides more rotational movement and "reach" than a low underarm when using a set-in sleeve. The underarm should not be so high, however, that it is uncomfortable. The underarm of this test garment was too low, so I added fabric and then drew in the underarm placement that I wanted, connecting the underarm to the front and back crease. See pattern work on page 118.

25 The back armhole.

26 Establish the shoulder line placement, making the body look proportionate and balanced, with the shoulder seam in middle of arm and in a pleasing position at neck. As with the armhole placement, this is largely a judgment call.

27 Establish a neckline. For a basic pattern that will be used as a block or sloper, the base of the neck is a useful reference point. Here, the front neck is drawn.

28 Transfer the fitting changes to the pattern, adjust the pattern, make a new mock-up, and fine-tune the fit. Once a test garment is fitting well, you can begin to fit the sleeve.

PATTERN WORK EXAMPLES

See Altering Patterns for basic pattern-making techniques, page 61.

Back Armhole Adjustments

The red tick marks taken from the muslin indicate the new back armhole seam line. Note that paper was added in order to raise the underarm (**A**).

The completed pattern with the new back armhole (**B**).

Center Back Curvature

The red tick marks taken from the muslin indicate the new center back seam line (**C**).

The center back seam blended. To provide more ease through the mid-back, blend the original seam to the new seam line just a few inches (cm) above the waist (**D**).

Adding Waist-Fitting Darts

The black tick marks taken from the muslin indicate the waist-fitting dart. It's best to have an equal amount of intake on each side of the dart. To do this, draw a straight line between the mark that indicates the top of the dart and the mark that indicates the bottom of the dart (**E**).

Measure the total dart intake at one set of the tick marks (**F**).

Divide the total intake in half, and mark one-half of the intake on each side of the center line of the dart. Repeat for all sets of tick marks (**G**).

Blend the new tick marks to complete the waist-fitting dart (**H**).

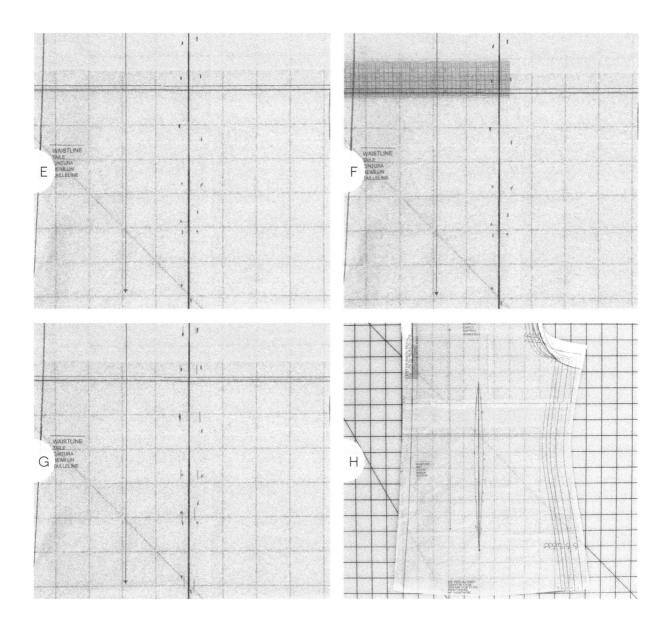

BODICE WITH SHOULDER PRINCESS LINE

Shoulder princess lines nicely accommodate all bust sizes and shapes, and are useful to fit a wide variety of back issues as well.

STYLE/FITTING CONSIDERATIONS OF PRINCESS LINES

Princess lines in general are extremely effective fitting tools, because the seam line goes over or near the apex of the bust. In addition to their effectiveness in obtaining a good fit, they are easy to modify to achieve a garment that is flattering visually. Princess lines start at the hem, go over the bust, and can end in a number of places on the upper body.

Shoulder princess lines (**A**) intersect the shoulder seam, usually at the midpoint, and the vertical line is visually slimming.

Neckline princess seams are not frequently found in commercial patterns, but they also produce a pleasing vertical line. Changing where the princess line intersects the neck can make the bust appear smaller (**B**) or fuller (**C**).

The position of armscye princess lines also carries a visual impact, making the bust appear rounder (**D**) or making the upper torso appear longer (**E**). The need to join a concave and a convex curve in armscye princess lines can make them difficult to sew; raising the intersection point on the armhole makes sewing easier.

If a princess line does not go over or very near the apex of the bust (**F**), the bust area cannot be fit effectively. With princess lines that fall to the side of the bust, a short dart completes the fit and produces an interesting style variation.

A

B

C

D

E

F

PROCESS OF FITTING THE BODICE WITH SHOULDER PRINCESS LINE

1 The bodice front. Although the garment does not close over the bust, the shoulders fit well. Rather than assuming that the client needs a larger size, first assess how the rest of the garment fits.

2 When viewing the garment from the side, note the excess fabric in the back above the HBL. Also note the drag lines emanating from the bust and pointing toward the waist and hip. The combination of these issues suggests that a full bust is the reason the bodice did not close at center front.

3 Viewed from the back, the bodice looks snug across the upper back but otherwise not tight. Note the low left shoulder.

4 Release the front princess seams over the bust. The princess seams spread, allowing

the center fronts to match. Clip the neckline and front armholes to eliminate tightness.

5 Releasing the front princess seams allows the bodice back to relax.

6 Note the excess fabric below the shoulder.

7 Pin out this excess fabric in a wedge. Begin to pin the princess seam working from the top downward. Note the bagginess on the side front panels.

8 Release the remainder of the front princess seams. The difference in length between the front panel and the side front panel is typical when making a full bust adjustment.

(continued)

9 Slash the front panel above the HBL, and add a piece of fabric to lengthen the upper portion of the bodice, bringing the HBL into position so that it matches the HBL on the side front.

10 In order to pin the front princess seam over the bust, assess where the extra front girth needs to be added. The side seam is straight and there is no strain. This indicates that all of the extra fabric needs to be added at the bust.

11 Add extra fabric and pin the princess seams to it, smoothing the mock-up fabric so that it is neither tight nor loose over the bust. Slip in a small shoulder pad on the low shoulder. This could have been done during an earlier step, but I chose to wait until the garment had really begun to settle on the client.

12 Once the extra girth for the bust is added, experiment with and place the new front princess seam. In your pattern work, use the new

princess seam placement to guide you in determining how much to add to each pattern piece.

13 Viewed from the side, the back HBL is low in comparison to the front. When the extra fabric was added to lengthen the bodice front (step 9), more length could have been added. However, because the garment is a bit snug over the buttocks, I chose to raise the back HBL a small amount.

14 The back HBL raised. Note the drag line emanating from under the bust going to the side seam at elbow level.

15 The drag line identified in the previous step can be eliminated by either increasing the dart intake (pinned on the client's right) or by adding a waist-fitting dart (pinned on the client's left).

16 If the client prefers a snug fit through the back, take in the back princess seams.

acknowledgments

Heartfelt thanks to everyone who helped in many different ways:

A Fabric Place

Michael Bearman

Rae Cumbie

Michael DeFilippi

Blondell Howard

Henrietta Jones

Tovah and Nick Kopan

Marcie Levendusky

Annie McCarty

Douglas Preston

Bob Ross and Lorraine Ferland

Elisabeth Stewart and family

Krista Veblen

about the author

Sarah Veblen is a custom fashion designer who focuses on teaching, creating clothing, and writing. Making clothing for her private clientele for more than twenty-five years, Sarah specializes in fit, innovative pattern design, and quality garment construction.

Sarah has been a long-time and active member of the Association of Sewing and Design Professionals, the American Sewing Guild, and the Haute Couture Club of Chicago. She has written more than twenty articles for *THREADS* magazine, has contributed to numerous other publications, and has a series of fitting videos with Taunton Workshops. She collaborated with Fit for Art to develop the *Eureka! Pants that Fit* pattern. Dedicated to promoting sewing at all levels, Sarah teaches at her studio in the Baltimore area, online for PatternReview.com, and as a guest lecturer for various sewing groups and organizations.

index